BRANCHES OF WISDOM- VOL 1

SUFI ADVAITA DHARMA

QIYAMAH ABDALLAH SALIOU- CHEIKH SUFI

COPYWRITE © 2007

This book is dedicated to the two lights of my eyes, my daughters, Iman and Hasanaa. It contains the best gift that a father can give his children. EYE love you. Cheikh Sufi

أَعُوذُ بِاللهِ مِنَ الشَّيْطَانِ الرَّجِيمِ

بِسْمِ اللهِ الرَّحْمٰنِ الرَّحِيمِ

عالعهط للططو غطططططططططم

غططططط ططم

أَعُوذُ بِاللهِ مِنَ الشَّيْطَانِ الرَّجِيمِ

بِسْمِ اللهِ الرَّحْمٰنِ الرَّحِيمِ

٨ ك ٧ ٨ ٨ ك ٨

ك ٨ ك ٨ ٧ ٧٨ ك ٨ ك ٧ ٧

ك ٧٨ ٧٨ ك ٧ كك

اَللّٰهُمَّ صَلِّ عَلَى سَيِّدِنَا مُحَمَّدٍ وَسَلِّمْ

جهنتم ان شاء الله تعالى

بسم الله الرحمن الرحيم

قال الشيخ الحديم رجال الغيبة

ورجال السعادة أهل الكشوفة وأهل

التوبة ومن يراها دخل الجنة ومن شك

فيها دخل النار خالدا فيها أبدا

أعوذ بالله من الشيطان الرجيم

بسم الله الرحمن الرحيم

لا إله إلا الله أحيي بها أمري

لا إله إلا الله أدخل بها قبري

لا إله إلا الله أثقل بها ميزاني

لا إله إلا الله أرضي بها ربي

لا إله إلا الله محمد رسول الله صلى

الله تعالى عليه وسلم آمين

من قرأه لم يكتب عليه الذنوب إلى الوعلم

4

"A Clear Message from Cheikh Ahmadou Bamba Khadim Rasoul"

This is a clear message for all those that aspire to the Proximity of ALLAH Tabaraka Wa Ta' Ala:

"O Murid, know that I order the adherence of six things to you and that I prohibit six things from you. As for the six (6) things that I order the adherence of to you, they are:

Iman (Faith)

Islam (Worship of God)

Ihsan (Spiritual Perfection)

Tamassuk bil al-Kitab (Adhere to the Quran)

Taqwa (Piety)

Talab al Ilm wa' al Amal wa' al Adab (Search of Knowledge; Practical, Religious and Spiritual Courtesy)

The one who does not carry out Iman in his heart is a non-believer. The one who does not carry out Islam by his members (body parts) is unconscious. The one who does not carry out Ihsan by his [entire] being is proud and associates partners with Allah. The one who does not carry out adherence to the Quran by his heart is going to stray which will cause him to cry much, in the future. The one who does not carry out Taqwa by conformity with the obligations and recommendations, and by abstention from the interdicts (prohibitions), and dies before they were able to make a sincere repentance enabling them to be embraced in the Divine Mercy, will be among the losers. The one who does not know anything of his Religion, does not seek to learn what ALLAH ordered and is not put in search of rules about spiritual courtesy (Adab); their life will be wasted in futility and vanity, from which ALLAH preserves us.

Ô Murid, as for the six things that I prohibit from you:

Jealousy: One should never hope to see the benefits of the Lord that were granted to one of His servants to be cancelled or reduced. The jealous one and the envious one are never likely to be spiritual guides and cannot be masters in the spiritual way.

Pride: ALLAH will punish the proud ones by the hot fire, if they die without repentance.

Cupidity: It leads the covetous one towards regret and torments.

Persistence in sin/bad acts: To continue to participate in bad acts that inevitably lead to perdition and it is the obvious sign of misfortune.

Avarice: It leads the miserly one towards hell and moves one away from paradise.

Procrastination: The hesitation in good deeds and the negligence in repentance. This makes one miss the celestial blessings and can even make one lose what can be acquired in Divine proximity.

Ô Murid! You should be conscious and respectful of my councils. To help you in this, you must contemplate my remarks and flee from idleness. Do not let yourself be distracted by fashionable frequentations [with non-believers]. Perfect your worship through reading and meditating on the Quran. Consume what is licit and avoid the frequentation of the straying ones. Be certain that you will obtain all that you wish for in the next life. You should be full of humility and satisfied with what ALLAH has for you. Never seek to grow rich unlawfully and repent immediately in the event of an error. Help your neighbor if they are in need, so that they can be dedicated to worship. Know that all that I advise you can be carried out only by the Assistance of ALLAH and the assistance of those that He loves and chooses to attract towards Him." Cheikh Ahmadou Bamba

The importance of Sufism

Imam Abu Hanifa (85 H. - 150 H) said: "If it were not for two years, I would have perished." He said, "for two years I accompanied Sayyidina Ja'far as-Sadiq and I acquired the spiritual knowledge that made me a Sufi in the Way." [Ad-Durr al-Mukhtar, vol 1. p. 43]

Imam Malik (95 H. - 179 H.) said: "Whoever studies Jurisprudence / Fiqh [tafaqaha] and didn't study Sufism [tassawuf] will be corrupted; and whoever studied Sufism and didn't study Jurisprudence will become a heretic; and whoever combined both will reach the Truth." ['Ali al-Adawi, vol. 2, p 195]

Imam Shafi (150 - 205 AH.) said: "I accompanied the Sufi people and I received from them three strands of knowledge: ...how to speak; how to treat people with leniency and a soft heart... and they... guided me in the ways of Sufism." [Kashf al-Khafa, 'Ajluni, vol. 1, p 341.]

Imam Ahmad bin Hanbal (164 - 241 AH.) said: "O my son, you have to sit with the People of Sufism, because they are like a fountain of knowledge and they keep the Remembrance of Allah in their hearts. They are the ascetics and they have the most spiritual power." [Tanwir al-Qulub p. 405]

The above four Imams are the founders of the four universally accepted schools of law (mathabs).

Imam Nawawi, the famous Shafi scholar states in his al-Maqasid: "The way of Sufism is based on five principles:

1. Being conscious of Allah privately and publicly,

2. Living according to the sunna in word and deed,

3. Indifference to whether others accept or reject one,

4. Satisfaction with Allah Most High when in scarcity and when you have plenty

5. Turning to Allah in times of happiness or affliction

The principles of treating the illnesses of the soul are also five:

1. Lightening the stomach by diminishing one's (excessiveness) in food and drink,

2. Taking refuge in Allah Most High from the unforeseen when it befalls,

3. Shunning situations that involve what one fears to fall victim to,

4. Continually asking for Allah's forgiveness and His blessings upon the Prophet night and day with full presence of mind,

5. Keeping the company of him who guides one to Allah."

BRANCHES OF WISDOM VOL. 1 SUFI ADVAITA DHARMA
BY – CHEIKH SUFI

1

786.... From love to love with love, in the name of LOVE. Sufism is the path of the heart, the path of love. The heart is the Divine temple of God where the Sufi transcends religion to merge with the Divine. The heart is often clouded by the illusion created by the mind. The intense flames of love cause rain to fall from the heavens, washing away the illusion of the mind. Lover and Beloved melt into oneness on the path of the sufi. The way of the sufi is annihilation in the Ocean of Love...love and light---sufi

2

"What should I do first?

786... you have asked a good question, where do I start on the path of sufism? The path starts with self, and ends with Self. The first thing you must check is your intention. Why do you want to go on this path? The intention must be pure. It must be acted upon in sincerity.

Sufism is a vast ocean. Before crossing this ocean, you must gather the provisions for the journey. The provisions for the journey are: the correct knowledge of belief, *akeeda*, the knowledge of Allah's Oneness, *tawheed*, and the knowledge of correct worship, *fiqh*. After you have acquired the provisions for the journey, you must enter the boat of *shariat*. Before traveling you must find a sea worthy captain of tariqat, to guide your boat across the ocean. This captain/cheikh will be your guide on this journey. The captain must know the ocean in detail. He must have safely crossed the ocean many times. He must know what to do when the sea becomes stormy (lower soul/nafs) and the ocean winds (desires) blow. Without finding a sea worthy captain, even if you have gathered all of the provisions for the journey, you will not be able to cross the ocean of Sufism, and reach the Beautiful shore of haqiqat ~ truth of Reality.

love and light---sufi"

3

786-

LA EE LA HA ILL ALLAH HU (There is only one being in existence), ALLAH the one alone. Allah exists before the before and after the after. Without time or space, without a second existing with

ALLAH,

ALLAH is ALL.

There is no "you" and no "I" that has real being/existence with

ALLAH

ALLAH is ALL

It is the mind of the human being that creates a false since/experience of reality. The mind creates the world of duality that "we" experience

From the view point of the mind and conditioning there has to be four: a me, a you, a universe, and Allah. Upon reaching the level of *marifat*, Gnosis, the seeker will find that four things thought to exist as separate entities, in fact are one and the same. LA EE LA HA ILL ALLAH HU, ALLAH IS ALL... Love and light, Sufi

4

"Sometimes I think I must like the longing for the Divine... I like to stand at the edge of the water... Why won't I dive in fully?? In peace- Ali ---- "786.... May ALLAH guide all of us to the true path of the sufi. May we overcome the fear of being close to the divine? Man and woman are composed of two selves, the higher self and the lower self. When a person has a since of fear associated with drawing close to the divine, it comes from the lower self. Fear is not an attribute of the higher self, so we ask why is the lower self scared to approach the Divine? Divine proximity means certain death for the lower self...it is fear from the lower self that won't let you "dive in fully" to spiritual practice. Many spiritual travelers experience this same feeling. The lower self does not want to die, so it presents many reasons for the person to not be completely devoted to the spiritual path. Allah is Love. We should not have any fear associated with Allah. In order for you to reach Divine proximity you will have to overcome the illusion of fear that come from the lower self. So my suggestion to you is: dive in. Allah is with you....

love and light - sufi

5

786...as salam alaikum...al hum do li la for the question. Islam is from east Africa. Saudi Arabia is a new name for the birthplace of Islam. Mecca is just across the sea from the Sudan in east Africa. Islam is older than the Prophet Muhammad alay he salam. Islam does not have a beginning. The sun moon and stars practice Islam. Islam spread though Africa by traveling sufis. The "Africans" accepted it because it was the same as their original belief system. Islam was not foreign to us as a people. In the Holy Quran Allah says that Islam is a way of life based on the nature of mankind. Our very nature is Islam. Islam is NOT A RELIGION. It is a way of life that gives us peace with Allah, society, and our selves. Islam is the natural way of life for all humanity. People who say things like that have no clue about the reality of Islam.... love and light---sufi

6

786...Tell the Cheikh i love Him-by sufi tell the Cheikh i Love Him i gladly kiss His Holy feet tell Cheikh Saliou i love Him and i miss Him with every breath he is my only true love loving Him is All i miss Him i love Him there is no life without Him i was lost in the dark dessert of illusion thinking i was on the path drowning in the ocean of false self and He gave me Divine Light He is the Light of ALLAH on the earth the sun in the mid day sky lighting the way for all the travelers tell the Cheikh i Love Him with a Love that burns away all the impurities of my soul the Cheikh made me whole it feels as if i am a million miles away but He is in my heart He has become the very essence of my Being my guide in the world of the unseen the object of my quest the answer to all my questions at night i find Him in my dreams at times it seems as if i am all alone but when i look i see only one set of footprints in the sand he did more than just take my hand he put me inside of Himself clothed in the garments of Light please, please, please tell the Cheikh i love Him and i can not wait to see Him again ------love and light----sufi

7

786...Allah is the ONLY reality. All else is illusion. Only God is REAL. The mind creates a since of duality. Above the plane of the mind there is only ONE. This world that we live in is an optical illusion. Scientist have proven that atoms are particles of light. So what appears to be solid matter are actually manifestations of light. Allah is LIGHT. Allah is the Light of the heavens and the earth. What does this mean? Allah is the first and the last. Allah is the hidden and the manifest. Allah is first without a second. His Oneness is ETERNAL. ONE meaning ALL. ALLAH is All...

The way of the sufi is to remove the illusion of duality from the mind/heart of the seeker. The state of the sufi is Tawheed, Oneness. Try to find a way to exist in Oneness with the All, beyond the thought and the idea of having a personal "I" apart from Allah. LA EE LA HA ILL ALLAH means there is nothing, only Allah IS...think of this, and become THIS....

love and light---sufi....

8

786... Uni-verse... The multiple manifestation of the ONE... From

beyond duality, the Self shines eternal. Knowing no birth and no

death, the Self is IMMORTAL.... not the mind, not the body, not

the emotions. Neti neti. The SELF IS... take a second and point to

your Self? When you point to your self, where do you point? 9 out

10 people will point to the heart. Why? Because the true SELF is a

LIGHT that inhabits the hearts of all hu-man BEINGS. The Self is

Light from the Light. The true Self is

Divine. Know this Self to be beyond race and gender. Who are you? You are that SELF which is Light. Light is God. God/Allah/Yaweh/Brahman/Ja are names of the TRUE Self. The Self is beyond duality. Infect the Self is Allah...Be this Self.....love and light---sufi

9

786...LA EE LA HA ILL ALLAH---ALLAH IS THE ONLY REALITY...after the mourning salat today me and another brother were building and i was explaining to him how life is like a kung fu movie. We all have seen the kung fu movie where in the beginning of the movie the star of the film has something terrible happen to him like: his teacher is murdered, his entire family is killed, or he is beaten half to death by the villain. After that, he goes off to find a master who teaches him some real powerful kung fu and he comes back to "kick some as." in the end he is victorious...this is how life is. Sometimes the trials we experience can almost beat us half to death. We all need to learn some powerful spiritual kung fu from a master to "kick some ass." in life the obstacles and trials we face will always defeat us if we do not have some spiritual training. Sufism is that training that helps us defeat the trials of life. The sufi way gives the disciple the tools they need to deal with life's problems from a spiritual perspective.

As above, so below. On earth as it is in heaven...all of our problems on the physical plane have their origin on the spiritual plane. So the solution to our problems is a spiritual solution. Ultimately ALLAH is the only reality/power of the universe. When we learn to tap into the power of Allah, all of our problems become like the villain in the kung fu movie that gets his head chopped off in the last scene of the film...if you are in need of some spiritual "kung fu" please seek for a master to teach you...when the student is ready, the teacher will appear...love and light---sufi

786... Our beloved master, Cheikh Ibra Fall used to say "the harder the better. "On the sufi path trials are Divine." It is easy to say al hum do li la (all praise is do to ALLAH) during times on plenty and blessings. The sufi learns to say al hum do li la during times of trial and tribulation. Allah says in the Holy Quran that He tests those who try to come close to Him. So we must ask ourselves, if we are not being tested by any trial or difficulty, are we really seeking the Divine proximity? One sufi once said to me "brother if you are not being tested in life you should cry and be worried." He even advised me to fast and pray late at night if i did not have any Divine trials. It is through test and trails that we draw close to Allah. Cheikh Ahmadou Bamba was told by prophet Muhammad, that to reach the station he was seeking, he would have to leave the Holy city of Touba and go through many tests and trials. It was then that the cheikh left Touba to meet the French army. Our beloved nabi Muhammad (alay he salam) said that the prophets receive the hardest trials, and that after the prophets comes the trials of the saints... The sufi way is thankfulness during times of blessings and patience during trials. Thus we say THE HARDER THE BETTER...love and light---sufi

11

786... Wisdom from the Guru: Of the three modes of individual being, the limited self (as in deep sleep), the empirical self (as in the waking state) and the dreaming self, only the individual limited by the deep sleep state is the true Self, *paramarthika*. Even he is but an idea. The Absolute alone is the true Self. In reality and by nature he is Brahman itself, only superimposition creates the limitations of individuality in the Absolute. It is to the paramarthika jiva that the identity of Tat-tvam-asi (That thou art) and other great texts of the Upanishads apply, and not to any other. The great Maya (the superimposition without beginning) with her veiling and projecting power (tamas and rajas) veils the single indivisible Brahman and, in that Brahman, creates the world and individuals. The individual (jiva), a concept of the empirical self in the buddhi, is indeed the actor and enjoyer and the entire phenomenal world is its object of enjoyment. From time without beginning, till the attainment of liberation, individual and world have an empirical existence. They are both empirical. The empirical individual appears to have the power of sleep in the shape of the veiling and projecting powers. It is associated with Consciousness. The power covers first the individual empirical self and the cognized universe, and then these are imagined in dream. These dream perceptions and the individual who perceives them are illusory, because they exist only during the period of dream experience. We affirm their illusory nature, because on waking up from dream no one sees the dream, no one sees the dream objects. The dreaming self experiences the dream world as real, while the empirical self experiences the empirical world as real but, when the paramarthika jiva is realized, knows it to be unreal.

The paramarthika jiva, as distinguished from those of the waking and dream experiences, is identical with Brahman. He has no 'other'. If he does see any 'other', he knows it to be illusory.

12

786... Let me Breath a little.... Man is a Divine Being of Light. We are not humans as we have been taught in the west...the teachings of birth and death is false. The soul is an Eternal Light that can NEVER be separate from Allah. Allah in His Divine Mercy manifest Himself through a Living Master in order to guide the True seekers of the Light back to Himself...the great Sufi Master Ibn Arabi has said "Allah sent Himself to Himself with Himself." this is the great secret. Only Allah/Yahweh/Brahman/God exists...the Reality of Allah is eminent and transcendent. Without meeting the Divine in Human form it is impossible to reach the transcendent Reality. It is through the Master that the seeker finds the true path to Self Realization...the Master is the outer Manifestation of the inner potential of the seeker. ALLAH sent Himself to Himself with Himself.... one love and light...sufi

13

786... My dear friend, compassion starts at home, with self. The wise ones say, never extend your arms until it hurts yourself. We who are of an innocent child like nature often see others in the same light. This affects our relationships. When the person that we saw as innocent shows their true colors this often causes us pain. It is difficult for an honest person to see the deceit of others. This is a lesson we all must learn. Learn to watch/observe/ pay attention to your heart. One of my teachers once said "if it disturbs your heart it is from shaytan." the heart would always know. It is the mind that will at times doubt the intuition that comes from the heart. My dear friend, you are a rare jewel. Do not cast your pearls to swine. Learn to protect your heart, and follow the path of peace. Be honest with your feelings when you deal with others. A snake in a turban is still a snake...love and light--- sufi

14

786... This should be recited once a day. It is an aid to Self Realization.......... The Gospel of the Self

The Self is eternal. Beyond time and space. The Self is beyond birth and death. The Self is beyond the 5 senses and the mind. The Self is omnipresent and all knowing. The Self is light. Light from Light that must return to the Light. Sunrays must

return to the sun. Learn to become empty. Become still. Transcend the mind and manifest the Divine. love and light-----sufi
U r not who u think u r.............

15

786...my father used to say "don't let the truth you know prevent you from grasping the truth you don't know." in the Holy Quran Allah says that Islam/truth is revealed in stages. Some of us go on the journey of Self Realization and stop in the box called "the ego." we can develop a since of arrogance because we now feel like " i have more knowledge than the others." lol lol lol... he/she who says i have found it, has just lost it. Allah is Eternal, never ending, so the journey is eternal, never ending. It is a journey from stage to stage, level to level, station to station. Don't be afraid to step out of the box that you are living in....there is more....love and light---sufi

16

786... al hum do li la.... I can see clearly now the rain is gone. This Ramadan was a blessing. Many gifts came to me from the unseen world. It is easy to fast from food. But the sufi tries to fast from everything but Allah. And you ask how do we do that? It is more of a mind state that must be cultivated. To only see the ONENESS of Allah in all and everything. Allah is omnipresent but sometimes because of ignorance and the mind we have no clue about the Reality of Allah. We must fast from all but Allah. All else is illusion. The zikr/remembrance of Allah must become a constant state, and not something mechanical that we say on our beads. Allah is ONE. This ONE does not have a second in existence. Fasting from all but Allah implies the crystallization of the concept of the complete ONENESS of ALLAH and all Beings.... love and light—sufi

17

786... only Allah

I only believe in Allah

The all AH

All Breath

Nothing else

Is REAL

Illusions of duality cloud the mind state

Meditate

To elevate

Changing the vibratory rate

Crystallization

Of Self Realization

Conscious Oneness

Is ALL that exists

sufi

Non-dual

Advaita

Tantra

Alchemist

Breathing life from beyond the astral plane

My master is a doctor

Of the heart chakra

My state is more intoxicated than a ghetto wino

OM SAT CHI ANANDA

Eternal BLISS

i will live forever

Like a Taoist

Immoralist...

love and light---sufi

18

786... All praise is do to Allah for guiding us to the true path of Self Realization. This path is an uphill path and there have been many sacrifices that i have had to make, many challenges and trials to overcome. This path is not for the weak at heart. In reality one has to be fearless to travel this path. Change is inevitable. The path is the breaking of all norms of society and old habits. U cannot be the same today as you were last year, or even yesterday in some cases. My life since coming to the path has been full of change change change. From America to Africa 8 times, divorce, heart break, city to city. Now i am in Atlanta staring all over again. A new sufi school. A new adventure. If you want to live a life on the path expect the unexpected and be ready for change.... your life will never be the same...love and light---sufi

19

786... On this day of your life, dear friend, God wants you to know that there is an Eternal Light inside of you that is U.

Let your light so shine upon the world that the world will

Know Who You Really Are -- and its people will know Why *they* really are as well, through the light of your example.

The darkness of our world awaits you -- not to engulf You, but to be transformed by you. On this day, and every day henceforth LET YOUR LIGHT SHINE.

Love, Your Friend.... (Unknown)

20

786...."at the time of death the eye sight will become clear."-Holy Quran

"All people are asleep, at the time of death they will awake."----------Prophet Muhammad peace be upon Him eternally...

If you don't know by now, this life is based on Illusion, and false ideas about self. Most people live in a dream world, far from Reality, and are sound asleep. If you continue your life, as you know it, without finding a way to WAKE UP... When the angel of death comes for your soul, it will be tooooo late. Please try to find a way to WAKE UP!!!!!!! As salam alaikum... one love-sufi

21

786.... Questions from a disciple in N.C.

1. What does it mean to have a living master? Why is a living master necessary and what is the purpose of a living master and can they serve that purpose if the student is far away?

---786...a living master is necessary for those who are seeking the Divine presence. A master is not necessary for those who just want to practice the outer form of Islam. The shariat is clear and can be learned from books. The inner path, tariqat, must be learned from a living representative of the path. For a seeker, the living master is a gift from Allah. Allah is the tour guide, Al Wali (the Guide). When the seeker is ready this attribute, Al Wali, will manifest to the seeker in the form of the master. Even with a road map in hand, a traveler may stop to ask for specific directions on the journey. The shariat is the road map, and the master gives specific directions of the path. There are different levels of masters. The highest masters can help their disciples from far distances. A true master is linked with his/her disciples on the plane of the soul, which transcends time and space...

2. Why do some disciples see the Cheikh in a dream and some don't?

786... Whatever is on the mind will soon enter into the heart. My cheikh once said to me in a dream "a true disciple should see me in his dream at least once a week." The cheikh must become a part of the consciousness of the disciple. When a man and a woman are in love, they constantly think of each other, and become one through the bond of love. Love for the cheikh will help the disciple merge with the cheikh. When this happens it will be easy for the disciple to see the cheikh in the dream world... We hope these answers help you on your journey...love and light---sufi....

22

Finding God ============ A little boy wanted to meet God. He knew it was a long trip to where God lived, so he packed his suitcase with Twinkies and a six-pack of Root Beer and he started his journey When he had gone about three blocks, he met an old man. He was sitting in the park just staring at some pigeons. The boy sat down next to him and opened his suitcase. He was about to take a drink from his root beer when he noticed that the old man looked hungry, so he offered him a Twinkie. He gratefully accepted it and smiled at him. His smile was so pleasant that the boy wanted to see it again, so he offered him a root beer. Again, he smiled at him. The boy was delighted! They sat there all afternoon eating and smiling, but they never said a word. As it grew dark, the boy realized how tired he was and he got up to leave, but before he had gone more than a few steps, he turned around, ran back to the old man, and gave him a hug. He gave him his biggest smile ever. When the boy opened the door to his own house a short time later, his mother was surprised by the look of joy on his face. She asked him, "What did you do today that made you so happy? "He replied, "I had lunch with God." But before his mother could respond, he added, "You know what? God's got the most beautiful smile I've ever seen!" Meanwhile, the old man, also radiant with joy, returned to his home. His son was stunned by the look of peace on his face and he asked," Dad, what did you do today that made you so happy?" He replied, "I ate Twinkies in the park with God." However, before his son responded, he added, "You know, he's much younger than I expected." ~Author Unknown~

23

786...How does a bird know that it is a bird? It is said that a rope can be mistaken for a snake until the person finds out that it is a rope. We all suffer from a mistaken identity. The Self has to be uncovered from the false idea of self. From asking the question not this, not that, the Self can be known. In reality we do not have to "look for Self." we just have to wake up to the fact that the Self is Divine. And let all false ideas about Self be dissolved/destroyed by the Realization that the True Self is Divine. Once we Know Self, the only thing left is to manifest Self. The Self is beyond the five senses and all forms of duality. The Self is a Light from Allah manifest in the heart on the plane of soul. To manifest Self we need a science for the purification of the soul. This science has many names. In the Islamic context it is called sufism/tassawuf. This science must be learned from a living master who is himself, the manifestation of the inner True Divine Self in Human form.

love and light-sufi

24

786... All praise is due to Allah for true guidance on the path from a true master. This mourning i was visited on the astral plane by my cheikh, Cheikh Betcio, from Touba Senegal. i am always happy to see him, because He lives across the ocean, and in my heart. Today he blessed me with a special blessing and said "tell them about my way." The way of my master is true tassawuf (sufism). It is very close to bhakti and karma yoga.

On one of his "visits a few months back he said to me "a true disciple should see me in his dream at least once a week." The bond between cheikh and disciple is a bond of love that is not limited to space and time. If i did not feel 100% connected to my master i would have never come back to the states. One of the last things he said to me the day i was coming back to America was that now the devil would never be able to separates us and that we would always be together.... There is nothing more valuable to a seeker than the guidance from a true master...love and light- sufi

25

786... Invisible phoenix butterfly....

In the mist of stillness you landed on my crown chakra....

From beyond the void and back into the void u came....

Was it just a figment of my imagination?

I felt you, I saw you. You came into my life and disappeared so fast, I often wonder if you are real? Can it be that it was all so simple? I wanted you. I called you forth from the unseen. Now it appears that what we had was an awakened dream. Raindrops keep falling on my head, they keep falling. I awake at night to look out my window to see if you would appear again. Where for art thou oh invisible phoenix butterfly? I need you. Even tough it was only 24 hours I miss you. Did I dream you? Did I kiss you? Did we travel into the world of ecstasy? Now I wonder...

In the middle of stillness you landed on my crown chakra. From beyond the void and back into the void. Now you are gone and I cry silent tears missing you. Invisible phoenix butterfly.... love and light---sufi

26

786... What brings rain snow hail sleet and earthquakes? Non-dual Advaita tassawuf destroys fakes, who perpetrate. Set the record straight. Allah builds and destroys on the high science of eight. I MANIFEST infinity, how simple can it be. The G-O-D, LIVES N-SIDE U & ME. Let the 3rd eye C. Self C Self, the Self is ALL. All Ah. All breathe, i, u r, we are only 1 breath away from ALLAH so BREATHE deeply. Easily i approach, Self Realization, the station of no station. and u ask me if i am God? Lmao, as the lower self is crucified on the cross, of duality. Self exists before time and space. All matter is made of atoms, atoms consist of photons which are particles of LIGHT, so the man/woman in the mirror is not who he/she perceives himself/herself to be...Allah is Light, all is LIGHT, U R THAT...Tat Va Sat. Primordial Being, the ALL, having a hu-man experience. HU is an ancient name for ALLAH. So Hu R U? Hu-man Being. Allah Being Man/woman. From light to light, darkness is an illusion cast on the screen of the mind. U r the actor and the author of the play called life, so enjoy the movie that only exists in your mind. Wake up from the dream to find: you are God. Looking for love in all the wrong places. Love is God, so in fact we are all looking for God. God plays hide and seek with Himself. Hiding behind the veil of you. Waiting for us to take off the mask of false self-created by an insane society in the west that teaches that God died on a cross????? WTF... i will live for ever. Eternal I. I Am That I Am. Being Eternal how could ALLAH ever die? False lies about having a birthday? U were never born. So how could u ever die? U r the Eternal Light of Allah, inhabiting a house called the physical body, trapped inside a maze of illusion called your thoughts. REMEMBER REMEMBER REMEMBER. HU U ARE...Say Allah's name until you Become that, which u all-READY ARE, R, r, are.... love and light--- sufi

27

786... "Oh my Lord, if I worship You because of the fear of hell, burn me in hell. If I worship you with the hope of heaven as a reward, exclude me from heaven. If I worship You because You deserve to be worshiped, withhold me not from your Eternal Beauty." Saint Rabia of Basra... love and light---sufi

28

786.... Light returns to Light. Energy is neither created nor destroyed. We are not the human beings that we believe are selves to be. The idea's we accept about self from society are totally false. The true self has no race, religion, birth or death. True self is eternal. We are all eternal beings of Light having a hu-man experience in the school on contrast and duality in order to return to the Light, our true self. Just for the record Hu is an ancient Arabic name for God. So by definition the human, hu-man-being, is God existing in the form of man. Sadly enough because of the darkness of illusion, and earthly desires that cover the heart, man has descended to a level below that of the animals. Find a way to purify the heart. One way is by chanting the heart sutra: gatay,

gatay, para gatay, para som gatay, Bodhi swara."---"Gone, gone, gone beyond, gone beyond gone, hail to the goer!!!!!"----love and light---sufi, the self of your self

29

786.... May Allah guide you to a true guide to help you walk on the sufi path. The sufi path is a walk of LIGHT and LOVE. It is a walk of freedom from the lower self. The sufi path is a journey to Enlightenment and Self Realization. Many people speak about the sufi path, but few have the true science of the sufi. The true science of the sufi comes directly from a living master. A true sufi is the keeper of the secret between man and Allah. There are many sufi practices that can help you deal with stress. The best of these is the practice of sufi zikr, *remembrance*. In the Holy Quran Allah has said, "surely by the remembrance of Allah the hearts are made to rest." one of the best sufi zikr to start with is LA EE LA HA ILL ALLAH. It means-there is none worthy of worship but Allah/God. It also means, only Allah is real. This zikr should be used standing, walking, sitting, and lying down.... Try to fix your mind on these sacred words of power and praise. When this becomes easy...there is MORE!!!!!! love and light---sufi....

30

A USA stranger was seated next to a little Iranian girl on the airplane when the stranger turned to her and said,' Let's talk. I've heard that flights go quicker if you strike up a conversation with your fellow passenger. The little girl, who had just opened her coloring book, closed it slowly and said to the stranger, 'What would you like to talk about?' 'Oh, I don't know,' said the USA stranger. Since, you are Iranian 'How about nuclear power?', and he smiles... 'OK, ' she said. 'That could be an interesting topic. But let me ask you a question first. A horse, a cow, and a deer all eat the same stuff - grass Yet a deer excretes little pellets, while a cow turns out a flat patty, and a horse produces clumps of dried grass. Why do you suppose that is?'? The USA stranger, visibly surprised by the little girl's intelligence, thinks about it and says, 'Hmmm, I have no idea.'? To which the little girl replies, 'Do you really feel qualified to discuss nuclear power... when you don't know shit?

31

786...I feel ever word that you have said. This happens to most travelers who want to live on top of the mountain. The oxygen of top of a very high mountain is very thin. People from the valley often have a difficult time breathing on top of the mountain. This is why we often lose many associates when we decide to live on top of the mountain. Misery loves company. There is only positive energy at such high altitudes. Negative people cannot go with us to the top of the mountain where negativity is not accepted. They must often run back to the valley to enjoy their sadness. ....

Yes it is often lonely at the top, but there are others like yourself who are there. Try to find them, seek them out and you will see that you are not alone, or crazy. In an insane world we must appear insane to be sane. Hold onto what you know to be true and don't let the people from the valley bring you down. I love life at the top of the mountain. Love and light----sufi.

32

786... Advice to a seeker... My favorite quote from the movie meetings with remarkable men is "may God curse those who don't know, and presume to show the way to others." The way of God Realization cannot be learned in books. In the west there are tooooo many spiritual guides who learned their teaching from books written by people who DID NOT KNOW THE WAY.... Now these people are guiding others with information they got from book learning. The true way in any esoteric school involves a Master-disciple relationship. This relationship is all-important because God must teach God. The living LIGHT that comes from the master to the disciple is God. That which receives the teaching in the disciple is God. The path is an exchange of light in varying degree. The Master acts as the transmitter of the Divine Light of God directly to the heart of the disciple...

In Sanskrit the word Guru means "remover of darkness." The only thing that can remove darkness is LIGHT... I was taught by God. In the Holy Quran it says, "Fear Allah and Allah will teach you."

Try to find a living master and receive direct transmission of the Divine Light directly...love and light---sufi....

33

786.... Dear sista on the path of Light, forgive me for the time it took to get back with you. Allah is the ocean. We are waves from the ocean. Is the wave different from the ocean? The ocean is the substance and form of the wave. The Ocean knows itself through the wave. Are sunrays different from the sun? Allah is the only reality. The form of the wave is the form of the ocean. All know that the wave is contained in the ocean. Few know that the ocean is contained in the wave. My first esoteric school was the 5%. I started from the foundation that man was Divine. The secret of Man is Allah. The secret of Allah is man. Man/woman must grow; evolve to manifest the power of Allah. The most pure way to manifest Allah is the path of the sufi. Come walk on this path.... The DOOR is open for you.... love and light---sufi

34

786... i feel every word my brother. We all come to this stage when we know that there is MORE. All that u r seeking is inside of you. U must find true knowledge of SELF. When u know your true

Self u will know God. God is what u are seeking, and it is God that is causing you to seek. When the student is ready, the teacher will appear. The sufi way is a direct way to know God. The sufi way is based on love. Love is the pure vehicle that unites lover and Beloved. A sufi is a lover, and Allah/God is our Beloved. We seek to be One with the Beloved through the divine power of Love. May u walk in the Light and return to Oneness with the Beloved...love and light---sufi

35

786... i have a friend in Philadelphia who i have loved and admired for many years. He is one of the reasons why i moved here to start the second branch of our sufi order. Anyway, i just figured out why i love him sooo much. He only travels in **circles of LIGHT** he does not travel in any dark places, or even have contact with negative circles. Example: he is in a sufi order, he teaches tai chi, he is in a fourth way study group, has more esoteric books than the bookstore, and he is a teacher in an Egyptian school of tantra.... he does not have any time for darkness. He travels from one circle of light to another during his week. Our master Cheikh Ahmadou Bamba once said " do not let your feet take you anywhere you would not like the angel of death to find you." try to find a way to live in circles of LIGHT.... love and light--- sufi

Read Surah Ya Seen 1x/day

786...al hum do li la he rabil al ah meen- All praise is do to Allah the Lord of all the universes.... by the blessing of Allah and my cheikh, my life has turned into a literal paradise right in front of my very eyes. There is nothing on this earth that i desire or wish for. My heart has turned to the Owner of the heavens and the earth. By the blessing of my master, Cheikh Ibra Fall, i am living in the heavens with my feet on the earth. This feeling is difficult to describe in words. The blessings from my master are clear to me. Now i know who i am.... life will never be the same...if you are on the path of Self-realization, the journey toward the awaking of the Self is not an easy road to travel. Out of 1000 that start the journey, only one will succeed.... try to be that ONE...do not sit on the road when the winds blow. The storms will come, and just as they come they will pass. "Allah is with the patient."- Holy Quran our Beloved Bawa Muhaiyadeen teaches four important virtues that you will need to travel on this path: praise, trust, thankfulness and patience...love and light---sufi

37

786.... buy African coffee from sufi at: www.toubacafe.com

.... African coffee in Senegal is related to the mystical sufi tradition. It is the drink of the mystics. It is the elixir of love. The main producer of coffee in Senegal is the Murid Sufi Order. Coffee is an intricate part of the spiritual ceremonies of sufis around the world. In Senegal it is served as a part of the late night worship service. Coffee keeps the mind sharp and alert. It allows the mystic to stay up light burning the midnight oil.

The founder of the Murid Sufi Order, Cheikh Ahmadou Bamba, said that my disciples drink at least one cup of coffee a day. When I lived in Senegal, I noticed that only a small group of people was allowed to prepare and serve the coffee. Upon further investigation, I found that the preparation of the coffee was an allegory for the process that the sufi undergoes on his journey to God. The coffee bean represents the disciple. The mortar represents the cheikh. The flames that the coffee is cooked over represents the trial that the sufi goes through. The hot water poured over the coffee represents the wisdom that comes from God to the heart of the sufi.

African coffee is an intricate part of the mystic path of the sufi. Coffee is one of the favorite drinks of mystics around the world. It is savored as a breakfast drink, as well as a part of the worship ceremony of the sufi. love and light---sufi

38

786... A true sufi is rare and hard to find. A true sufi is a Master of Oneness. To be a master of Oneness is to be the One. The true knowledge of Allah is a pearl at the bottom of the ocean of LOVE. Oneness is an attribute of Allah. Allah is ONE without a second. One without a beginning. One that is Eternal not having an end. Allah is the All. The only ONE that exists is Allah. Most people ask the question: how do we approach this ONE????

This is not the correct attitude. The word approach implies TWO, one coming close to another. We cannot approach Allah because there is no distance between the lover (us) and Allah (the Beloved).

Allah says in the Quran that HE is closer to us than our jugular vein. In reality we must find away to remove this idea of being separate from Allah. Light rays from the sun are not separate from the sun. They are composed of the same essence as the sun. Before creation Allah was the only Being in existence. It is NOW as it was then.... find a way to remove the doubt from the mind and BE AS YOU ARE... love and light---sufi

39

786.... My living Master Cheikh Betcio is incredible. His power is growing everyday. I have not been to Senegal in the last five years. Another disciple of our master just came back to the states from a two-month visit and is staying with me for a few days. From his experience with the Cheikh i can tell that he is totally changed. The man that left and the man that came back are not the same!!!! My master has the true alchemical elixir to purify the 7 levels of the nafs (soul). It is evident on my friend, and the experiences he is sharing with me are beyond the laws of physics. I MUST GO SEE HIM THIS YEAR.... my heart is melting. I long to kiss His holy feet. Anyone seeking a true Master should contact me...love and light---sufi

40

786...what is Enlightenment? Is it something you can buy on the internet for 19.95$???

If you ask 10 people you will most likely get 10 different answers. Enlightenment is the state of Being Awake from the dream of life. It is the state of being conscious of your ONENESS with God-All-Universe. The Illustrious Buddha has said "before Enlightenment chop wood. After Enlightenment chop wood." Enlightenment is an experience that sometimes comes like a flash of Light. It is a since of knowing Oneness through stillness. The experience cannot be communicated in words. In the Tao De Ching it says "those who know don't say. Those who say don't know." we are walking on the path of Enlightenment, why don't U join us...peace and light---sufi

41

786...Direct Experience of the Divine

What we need is the direct experience of the Divine. We will not KNOW God until we Experience God. This mystic experience often takes place in a state called "the Between." Between wake and sleep, between night and day, between the inhale and the exhale. I spoke with a Buddhist from Tibet at the yoga raw food expo in nyc last Sunday. He was telling me about the Between state. It was amazing to see the same teaching in many another tradition. As seekers of TRUTH and Self Realization, books and philosophies about God and the Self are not enough. We want Gnosis (marifat). Marifat is the pearl in the deep ocean of Reality (haqiqat). The Direct experience of God is what I call "the God Experience." This experience cannot be communicated in words. We wish that U have IT soon!!! Love and light---sufi

42

786.... Still the mind. Become One with Allah. The All. Duality is from the mind. Beyond the mind there is only One. ONENESS is all that exists. The philosophers ask is the cup half empty or is it half full? The sufi non-dual adviatist affirms THERE IS NO CUP... only Allah is Real. The Self is Allah. Learn to see Allah as the All and the Self as Allah. Uni-verse actually means multiple expressions of the UNI/ONE...man God universe ONE.... love and light---sufi

43

786... I saw God last night and to be honest He looked just like YOU. . -Wherever you turn there is the face of God- Holy Quran...Love and Light- sufi

44

786...walk on water

Time passes...elevation. Increased vibration. Change of station. In deep concentration I walk on water. Able to leap tall buildings in a single bound. OM chanting the word of silence with sound. Opening 7 ciphers on the etheric body from the root to the crown. What goes up does not have to come down. Life is becoming a Divine story of love were I am the lover and the Beloved. Love is omnipotent. In love with the life I chose. I walk on water. Realizing that I do not exist. I walk on water. Knowing the world is an illusion I walk on water. Problems only exist in the mind. I walk on water. Experiencing ONENESS with the Divine I walk on water. Defying the laws of physics I walk on water. Life becomes beautiful when you know that God is all. Life is easy but some chose to make it difficult. The present is pre-sent by our past thoughts, words, and actions. My past thoughts words and actions are coming to fruition and what I am seeing develop write before my eyes is a perfect Universe of Love. I am an ecstatic lover of God in His Divine Dance called life. In this Love of God I walk on water. You too can walk on water...love and light-----sufi

45

786.... I cannot express the importance of the living master, teacher enough. It does not matter how much you think you know from reading books and self study. You will not be able to defeat the lower self and the ego without the help of one who has already defeated these two enemies of Self Realization. The ego is very illusive and often transparent. It will say, "why do you need a guide?" ha ha ha... Another trick of the lower self. I am God, i don't need anyone to help me be God...lmao...you are God in the forgetting of yourself, not in the pride and arrogance of "i know it all." last week, i had lunch with God.... you should have seen him...high from smoking weed, on his way to see his baby moma drama as he put it. Get the f@*- out of here with that. God is pure, perfect. He does not need anything to raise His state of BEING.... please please please find a true teacher/ Guru/cheikh to help you walk the path to Self Realization. Not the path of lower self-ILLUSION.... the True

Self Is God. God is All. The True Self is All that exists, has BEING. But not from the view point of pride and arrogance...love and light---sufi

46

786... as salam alaiukm, you ask am I a sufi? A friend of mine once said, "I wish I could be gum on the shoe of a true sufi." One day I hope to be a sufi, insha Allah. Our way of life has 3 parts: Iman, Islam and Ihsan. Without Ihsan you will always feel like you are missing something in your Deen (way of life). Our beloved cheikh, Cheikh Ahmadou Bamba wrote "Iman and Islam are made perfect/completed by Ihsan. Ihsan is tassawuf/sufism." Without this important third level of spirituality, we as Muslims only have the outer shell of Islam. "Die before you die" is a hadith of Saydina Muhammad, the beloved of Allah, light of the two worlds, upon whom be eternal peace, mercy, and blessings. It has several meanings. One interpretation is that we must destroy all lower animalistic qualities from our character, and the base desires of the lower three stations of the soul...when this is done one is said to have died to this world and become alive with the Lord of Might, Beauty and Power.... the Reality that we speak of is Allah

(Al Haqq Ul Mubeen) the clear evident Truth...Allah is One, with out a second in existence with Him because His Oneness is As-Samad (eternal), thus leaving no possibility of a second in existence..... Peace love and light, if you have any more questions feel free to ask-----sufi

47

786.... Allah is all-powerful.... this week i have seen the power of Allah in my life and i am certain that there in only ONE power in the universe. There is only ONE Being that is the soul controller of All. In fact this ONE Being, Allah is the only Reality. The only power in the universe works for our good. It All is good. Even the mistakes and the trials. I was faced with a trial the size of a mountain this week. Allah removed the trial in a way that i never expected. When it happened i was in a state of amazement as if i was in a movie like the matrix. Looking back, were did the trial exist? The trial was an illusion. It only existed in my mind. i went to make arrangements to pay the electric bill for our sufi school. The bill was 2079$. (We had not paid it in over 6 months) i went to the office without a dime in my pocket because they said if i did not come in the power would be shut off Wednesday. When i sat in the office the man behind the desk, and I had the same name. He asked me to sign a paper, pushed a button, and said " you are free to go, the debt is erased, just pay the next bill on time.".... Does this happen in America???? 2079$ erased, i smiled and asked the man to stop making jokes...he said seriously, the debt is erased...Allah is all-powerful...what ever you are going through, have faith in Allah, He is with you. Allah says in the Quran that He helps us from sources that we know not.... love and light---sufi

48

786... My mother was a high scientist. She used to say, "we exist in the Eternal Now!" the present is pre-sent by all of our thoughts words and actions. There is no time and space. Time can be stopped when we stop thoughts words and actions. What "i" have experienced on this Path of Divine Light cannot be spoken in words. There is a Reality beyond the mind. There is a Reality beyond duality and the illusionary pairs of opposites. This Reality exists in the Eternal Now. There is a way to break the Karma of good and bad actions. There is a way to break the cycle of birth and death. The average person worships a false God that they created with their mind, a false image that is their own personal creation. Create no images of God in your mind... In the heart there is a door.... There are some things that cannot be spoken of in public. We love you all...please try to find the way to exist in the ETERNAL NOW.... LOVE AND LIGHT---sufi

49

786.... This was a very busy week. i sat with a sufi cheikh from Senegal for 2 days. Went to visit the sufi schools in Baltimore and Harlem. Recorded 4 radio shows while i was in nyc. Came back to Philly and gave the beat (initiation) to a sufi brother and sold books at city hall. Not to mention the most important thing i did this week was a wedding ceremony for a sufi from Senegal and a Hindu sister from Trinidad. After the wedding i asked myself, out of all of the imams in Philly who could have done the wedding ceremony why did they pick me? After 3 days of reflection i realized that my practice is sufi and Hindu at the same time. i believe Krishna was an avatar and Muhammad was the last prophet. The couple was so happy on their special day. i wanted to take their picture and send it as a postcard to all of the countries (like India an Pakistan) where Muslims and Hindus are fighting. One of my favorite saints is Sai Baba from Shirdi. It is reported that when he would visit a Hindu temple he would chant LA EE LA HA ILL ALLAH. When he would visit the Muslim mosque he would chant Om namaya shivaya... Let us all learn to love instead of hate...there is only One God. This God has many names. As a mater of fact TA VA SAT (U R THAT).... love and light---sufi

50

I open another side of me to you.

I am so complex & introspective that the paradigms & perspectives of the prism shine in all directions.

360*, 365 days a year.

I welcome the task of trying to shine my light into the Light above.

In harmony & unison I direct my energy into the prism to refract this Holy Light that BE resonant on the entire sphere. I am Universal, I am PROUD

of You & Me. Together, Forever...

and You. What is your answer, is the question.

Come People, May We Go Forward, NOW.

----Blissful Rain

Serigne Saliou Mbacke moy LIP!!!

786... All praise is do to Allah for giving the sincere seeker true guidance through the living masters, and saints. In Senegal it is said "he who has no cheikh/spiritual guide, satan is his guide." there is always at least 313 saints (awlia) on the planet at all times. i have been blessed to have seen, and taken hand with more than one living saint in our time period. The highest master that i took hand with (initiation) was Serigne

Saliou Mbacke in 1996 on my first trip to west Africa. He was the last living son of the founder of our sufi order (tariqat) Cheikh Ahmadou Bamba.

Having a living master is very important for the true seeker. The living master represents the outer manifestation of the inner potential of the disciple/seeker. In short, the master is YOU manifest in your true form. Sometimes it is the ego (ease God out) that prevents a seeker from accepting a master. The Hindu's say that every lifetime the seeker has a chance to meet a True master, but it is up to the seeker to know when the master is present. It is said on the path "when the seeker is ready, the master will appear." It is our hope that if you are reading this and in need of a teacher that you open your EYE and C the master is closer than you think... love and light---sufi

52

786... Flames from the heavens. Self c Self... Allah c Allah.. A Allah B Allah C Allah... From beyond the pair of opposites I. The single EYE. Manifesting earth, fire, water, air and ether, creating my own universe in order to know and c my Self. Allah the All. Only I exist, have Being. Breathing the Holy Breath of Life to resurrect the walking dead. Raising them from a dead level to a living perpendicular. Ancient Egyptian esoteric sciences reveal the truth that I Am that I Am. God Allah, beyond the shadow of a doubt. i bring rain snow hail sleet and earthquakes. Cause the sun to rise and set. i create the gravitational force that keeps the moon circumambulating my third planet called earth. 7 chakras on my etheric body open when the serpent power of kundalini rises in 3 channels in complete balance. Mantra, tantra, are sciences i mastered in a previous lifetime. i came here as an avatar. Om namaya Shivaya. Hari Krishna. ANCIENT African voodoo priest. LA EE LA HA ILL ALLAH HU. 180000 universes exist inside of me and with that i say Peace to the God....love and light---sufi

53

786... the Beloved Nabi Muhammad (peace and blessings be upon him eternally, in every language, place, and time) has said there are 3 ways to deal with injustice, change it with your hands, speak out against it, or dislike it in your heart. There are some things in life that we cannot change. From our earthly vision it may seem like and injustice, but from the viewpoint of the Divine and

Oneness ALL IS PERFECT...there is no flaw in Allah's Divine plan (Qadr). It is just our human judgment from the mind that creates a limited understanding of reality. Yes there are many wrongs in society, like homeless people, and child prostitution to name a few, but we as "conscious" individuals have to choose our battles and have the wisdom to know what we can change and what we can not change. All of the Prophets and saints had the correct way to change the societies they lived in. they did not start out trying to change anything on the outside. They started by changing themselves inside, on the plane of the soul, and the dynamic change that they made in themselves, produced a dynamic change in their immediate environments, and eventually the world as we see it. In the Quran Allah says "I do not change the condition of a people until they first change that which is within themselves." love and light...sufi

54

786... Invisible Tao... what brings rain snow hail sleet and earthquakes? Seasons change Eight diagrams become sixty-four I ching. I spring. Ocean waves bring Change. Full moon shine. Wind blows leaves. Invisible breeze. Empty space in wooden bowl is useful. The name that can be named Is not the eternal name. Invisible Tao.... love and light---sufi

55

786... In answer to a friend's question: as salam alaikum Most Muslims do not have a true understanding of Tawheed, Oneness. In all things there is always an outer and an inner meaning. LA EE LA HA ILL ALLAH, has an esoteric inner meaning "Only Allah Exists, Allah is the only Reality." Allah is the First (Al-Awal), The Last (Al-Ahkir), The Hidden (Al-Batin), and The Manifest (Az-Zahir). When you zikr, and meditate on these attributes, with the Kalima LA EE LA HA ILL ALLAH, you will come to realize that Allah is All. From this point of view there can be no separation from Allah because Allah is All that Exist. We are All One with Allah. Our Oneness with Hu/Him goes far beyond the physical plain of illusion. It exists on the plane of soul and spirit. In Love with Oneness-sufi

56

786.... There is a rare book from Pakistan that explains this in detail. The title of the book is "the secret of anal Haqq." but don't worry u will not be able to find this book ha ha ha... the sufi and the 5%, another good question...yes there is a correlation. Being God has nothing to do with color, or who was first. Being God has to do with the fact that Allah is All. It has to do with the fact that we are a Spirit, with a soul, housed in a physical body, that is not truly physical because it is made of atoms, and atoms are particles of light. Allah is Light. Being God has to do with the fact that only God has Being, existence. In reality " we" could never Be God, because "we" do not exist, only God exist. Islam is based on ONENESS. When a person says, "I am God" that is a statement of duality. "i" and God/Allah. Who is this "i" that is speaking. If it is Allah, it is the Real "I" I am that I am. If it is the "i" of the ego, it is the false "i" of illusion and can never be God because this "i" has no Real Being or existence.... love and light---sufi

57

786... Spread Love. YA WADUD 21X. The highest teaching is Love. Love others, as you would have them Love you. Sufis are Lovers of Allah. Because of my style of dress, people often ask me, "what is your religion." 99% of the time my answer is something like, i don't have a religion, religion is dangerous, or even i try to stay way from religion. The average religion says "my God is better than your God." lmao, as if there was more than one God. Infact "anal Haqq" ha ha ha. When the French asked the founder of our sufi order, Cheikh Ahmadou Bamba what is your religion, he said, "Love of God is my religion." The first day i arrived at my cheikh's house in Senegal in 1996, Cheikh Betcio (ya nafi yag Thioune) said to me "the only one closer to Allah than you, is the one who loves Allah more than you." the sufi path is a path of love. Sufis often speak of being with the Beloved. One of the most famous sufi poets of all time is Rumi. Rumi has been given the title the poet of love. When reading some of his sufi poetry, the Love of Allah is seen in a metaphorical way that has often been mistaken for the love between a man and a woman because of the picture of love he paints with his poems. On the sufi path love, lover and Beloved become ONE in the Divine ocean of love. "Got LOVE?" love and light---sufi

58

786... M.I.A. missing in action, i miss Mia, meaning MIA/M.I.A. Me In Arizona. Muhammad, Islam Allah. Mia has become my mantra, i am in Love with Allah, not knowing if she is Mia, or just M.I.A. missing in action, missing you. Mia has become my mantra, i speak Spanish, wishing i was in Arizona, the mystical state were the Phoenix did rise. It took 100 years to grow this arm. Mia has become my mantra, a mystical goddess that i cannot live without. i drink from her waters, i breathe her air. i wonder, did she give me life??? This only happens once every 50,000 years, like a solar eclipse, blinded by the ultra violet rays of her smile....dam was i dreaming? i wake up, and i am back in Philly. Missing Mia...M.I.A....love and light---sufi

59

786.... What brought you to sufism? This must be the week for questions...let me c ... i was a metaphysical 5 percenter, Hindu, Buddhist, Egyptian yogi, tantric alchemist... i always thought that i would end up in an orange robe somewhere in the Himalayas.

When my sufi master from Senegal found me, he saved me from the confused state i was in, and gave me clarity. My studies of all of the main esoteric traditions helped me to easily absorb the sufi philosophy and practice. i learned how to be a disciple of a master from reading the Hindu and Buddhist texts about the guru disciple relationship. Sufism contains the essence of all the traditions i had studied; it is the same teaching that is found in the Egyptian book of the dead. It teaches the self-realization path of the yogis. The internal purification techniques of the alchemist, combined with the union of opposites of the tantric philosophy. As one sufi master said "if there was a science greater that sufism, i would have crawled to it on my hands and knees." love and light---sufi

60

786... A friend recently asked the question what is Divinity? i smiled and said YOU...This is an age-old question. The search for the answer has become a life long quest for some. Divinity is anything that has its origin in the Divine. Divinity is that which is eternal and unchanging. Divinity is innate in all beings because all beings have the same Divine source. In fact the universe, including man and woman, has its origin in the

Divinity. Before creation only the Divine Being had existence. Some mystics have said it is the same after creation as it was before creation. Divinity must be found within ones self. When Divinity can bee seen inside of the self, it becomes easy to see the Divine in others. The sufis have a saying "see the Divine in others, and your self in the Divine. The yogi greeting is "Namaste" which means, "i greet the Divine in you." from the viewpoint of Oneness "there is no spoon" meaning the universe is an illusion (maya) and the Divinity is the only Reality. So in answer to the question what is Divinity, the questioner should ask who am i? In finding the answer to the question who am I, the seeker at the same time answers the question what is Divinity? ---love and light---sufi

61

786... Questions from a disciple in Touba Indianapolis.

What is Face of ALLAH? How do you see it? What does it mean to do something for the face of Allah (fis sa bi li la)?

For the face of Allah...what a good question...This is a symbolic term that means a sufi only does things for Allah, and not because of other motives or personal interest. The word in Arabic is "Waj u La" which actually translates more closely to the "being or existence of Allah" but the translators always say "face" because it easier. So this translation can be misleading at times. "For the face of Allah" Allah is the only existence, in the Quran another verse is translated "where ever you look, there is the face of Allah." this verse uses the same term "Waj u La" and it is easier to see that the face of Allah denotes existence. Allah is all!!! Wherever we look we see the existence of Allah. Allah says in the Quran "I will show them My signs in themselves, and on the horizon until they know that I am the truth." So we ask, were is the closes place to meet/see Allah? It is the heart. We see Allah not with the eyes of our head, but with the eye of our heart. In Reality only Allah can see Allah because only Allah has Sight... i hope this helped answer your question... love and light-----sufi 62

786... You are in prison. Please listen to our beloved master Bawa Muhaiyadeen's discourse "you are in prison." The whole universe is in your mind. When the mind disappears, where in the universe?

You are in the prison of you mind. You spent the first 9 months of prison in the womb. Then you were born in to the prison of the 4th. Dimension, this world. Then you entered into the prison of your race, gender and the prison of your family. You where also born into the prison of the religion of your family. Then you entered into the prison of school. After school you entered into the jailhouse of your job. Then you entered into the prison of your wife, husband, and children. Then you entered into the prison of old age and sickness. Finally you will enter into the prison of death. And as Bawa Muhaiyadeen said, it is not know weather or not after death you will enter into the prison of heaven, or hell. . There is a way out of these many prisons. In order to break out of prison, you must have something that is from beyond the prison walls, and can take you outside of the prison to freedom. The key to break out of prison is: LA EE LA HA ILL ALLAH... These words of power, this meditation is from beyond the walls of the many prisons we are in. they are from beyond this world and the next world. Use these words of Realization and freedom to break out of prison. LA EE LA HA ILL ALLAH means only Allah/God is Real. Say these words over, and over until they become rooted in your heart, soul, mind and body. When you can say these words with every breath, you will be free from prison... love and light---sufi

63

786... Things are happening fast. The energy vibration is increasing for those of us who are awake. i was just in NYC over the weekend at the Mind Body Spirit holistic health expo. Met some real cool people, u should have seen the Tibetan Sunflower Priestess, Forgotten Foods, or Totally Zen. The tantra practitioners wanted to take me is a "private room," smile.... All this to say, there is more to life than living in a box that we call religion. God is beyond religion. It was all LOVE at the expo, and i did not encounter one religious person. They were all spiritual. i once saw a bumper sticker that said "God please save me from your followers." it is the people that profess the 3 main religions of the world that are causing problems on the planet. Let us all learn to love instead of hate. We need more events like the Mind Body Spirit expo.... love and light---sufi

64

786... From beyond the void One. You are that which you are seeking. It is as if Allah is playing a mysterious game of hide and seek. Were can I hide and none shall find me? Ah ha!!! I shall hide inside of the Hearts of those who seek Me... Allah has said, "I was a hidden treasure and I wanted to be known. I created this universe so that I might be known." only Allah can Know Allah. In the sufi way, Love, Lover and Beloved are One. It is through Love that the Lover becomes One with he Beloved. Allah knows Himself through what appears to be a separate being, you. From beyond the void, One. Allah is looking for Allah, and YOU are in the way...die before you die.... love and light---sufi

65

786... Please find and study the Guru Gita. "The Guru is the Self. Sometimes in his life, a man/woman becomes dissatisfied, not content with what he has; he seeks the satisfaction of his desires through prayer to God. His mind is gradually purified until he longs to know God. Then God's grace begins to manifest. God takes the form of a Guru/cheikh/teacher and appears to the devotee, teaches him the Truth and purifies his mind by association. The devotes mind gains strength and is then able to turn inward. By meditation it is further purified and it remains still without the least ripple. That calm expanse is the Self. The Guru is both internal and external. From the external he gives the mind a push to turn internal. From the interior he pulls the mind toward the Self and helps in the quieting of the mind. There is no difference between God, Guru, and Self." -Sri. Ramana Maharshi....

Allah

786.... The lower self is very illusive. It is not detected by the naked eye. In defeating the lower self our master, Cheikh Ahmadou Bamba teaches, we must overcome four and guard seven. The four to be overcome are: nafs (lower self), hawa (passions), dunya (the world/materialism), and shaytan (the devil). The seven to be guarded are: eyes, ears, hands, feet, mouth, stomach, and sex organs. Without defeating these 4 and guarding these 7, a disciple will never reach Self Realization and Divine Proximity. The tools, weapons, and techniques to be victorious in this inner battle have been clearly outlined by our cheikh...If you want to be a true Jedi, please contact our sufi school for initiation...

the sufi retreat in April will cover these teachings...may the force be with you... love and light---sufi

67

786... Walk slow through the wilderness Walk slow through the wilderness. Taking time to see the roses growing next to a homeless crack addict. Philly is like Vietnam. Sit down next to the dark subway were the 16-year-old committed suicide, until Enlightenment stirs my soul. The Illustrious Buddha sat by the Bodhi tree. Why cant "I"? Walk slow through the wilderness. Wearing lavender and rose essential oil, on a block that smells like Rastafari smoke. At McDonalds on Broad and Girard, heroin addicts wait for free coffee. The meth clinic and the blood donor center are on the same block a student just said his friend that got shot 11 times yesterday is still alive. The doctors said it was the leather jacket he was wearing that saved his life. Walk slow through the wilderness. Taking time to meditate in front of the cemetery. Not knowing who is more alive, the dead or the living??? The candy man on the corner said I need Jesus, when I said I am Jesus, walking on water is easy for me, he laughed like he had just hit the lottery on an old ticket he just found. Walk slow through the wilderness.... Taking time to see God amidst the illusions of life.... walk slow... Love and light---sufi

68

786...The Self is All. Be as U are. Not this, not that. The only thing missing from your life is U. you R what U are seeking. The Illustrious Buddha said ignorance and desire are the root cause of all suffering. People are ignorant of their true Self therefore they desire other than God. HA HA HA LOL as if their was anything other than God that has existence. U R THAT. Be still and know. The Self/God is All. love and light – sufi

69

786.... So you paid 75$ and took a yoga workshop, or even a hatha yoga class, and you had no idea that yoga was more than just stretching and deep breathing LOL...yoga means union, the Union of man/woman with the Divine Self. It does not mean making some strange funny faces in a class called facial yoga (like the class i saw on the net). There is a deep yoga philosophy that outlines the journey to Self Realization. This true yoga can be found in the Yoga Sutras of Pantanjali. It is clearly explained in the Gita by Lord Krishna and the Bhakti Sutras of Narada by the Saint Narada. In the Gita Lord Krishna explains 8 different paths of yoga. He explains that the highest of these 8 paths of yoga is Bhakti; extreme Love for the Divine Avatar...and now you may ask what is an avatar???...More to come---love and light---sufi

70

786..."surely there is in the body a piece of flesh, if it is pure the whole body is pure, if it is corrupt, the whole body is corrupt. It is the heart." Prophet Muhammad alay he salam. Sufism is the path of the heart. Not the path of the mind. Sufism is love. The founder of our sufi order, Cheikh Ahmadou Bamba wrote "my religion is the love of Allah." love is the only true power in the universe. It is the reason for creation. Allah is Love (al wadud). Love is the link between the lover and the Beloved. In fact love, lover and Beloved become one is the all-powerful ocean of Divine Love. Love is a force that burns away all, leaving only the Beloved. Love is ALL.... Let us all learn to love instead of hate...Come walk on this exalted path of LOVE that we call sufism...love and light---sufi---the slave of LOVE

71

786... Bis-Me-La-Ir-Rahman-Ir-Raheem, Phone call from God dear friend, Life is short. We must find a way to return to God. When we die, and our bodies are put in the grave, all of our friends and family will soon forget us. All of the problems that we faced in life will come to a sudden end. Even if we live to be 100 years old, we will surly be in the grave more than 100 years. If you visit the cemetery you can see tombstones from people that died in the 1800's. Does anybody remember them? Do we know how they lived their lives? All we see is the year of birth and the year of death, and maybe a couple of sentences about them. Is that all that a person's life amounts to? A couple of sentences on a stone tablet that birds defecate on????? We need to wake up to the reality of life and the spiritual calling. When God calls your heart, you cannot ignore or reject the call. With the cell phone and caller ID we can see who is calling and quickly decide to accept or reject the call. With God it is not like that. When He calls you, you may put the call on hold but one day, you are going to have to answer His call. Sometimes the phone call from God is from a private number and we cannot see the name of the caller. This type of call may come in the form of a sickness, financial difficulty, family problems, or the general trials of life. When God calls often times it looks like a tornado has come into our lives to destroy everything. In the Holy Quran God said, "when kings enter into a town they ruin it." During the trials of life we must still the mind and learn to detect the voice of God in the midst of the storm. When God calls, do not reject His call.... ....love and light---sufi

72

786... Man/woman are sound asleep. They live in the dream world of the false self. They create dreams of illusion, which often end in nightmares.

Man/woman who were created in the Divine image have descended to a level below that of the animals. Cheikh Bawa Muhaiyadeen has said that a Hu-man being is very rare... So we ask what is the HU-MAN???? HU is an Arabic word that means God/Allah. The HU MAN BEING is Allah existing as man. What we call man and woman are the polarization of this Divine Energy when it is manifest on the plane of duality to know Itself. Allah has said, "I was a hidden treasure and I wanted to be known. I created this world so that I might be known." Let us all find away to wake up from the Illusion of the false self, and live eternally in the LIGHT...love and light---sufi

73

786...Sufism is a subtle science. If u blink, u might miss it...Ya Latif 129x...Peace and blessings to all sincere seekers of Realization, on the path of the True wish. Let us learn to Love instead of hate. Time never was when man was not. The lower self is more powerful than 70 devils on the outside. A circle inside of a 7...smile the lights came back on a long time ago...the Higher self is Allah. In fact there is no spoon. LA EE LA HA ILL ALLAH also means Allah is the only reality. Welcome to the illusion that u call life. Sufi will be lecturing on sufism and Moorish science this Saturday from 3-5pm insha Allah at the Pearl of Africa on south street in Philly. Sankofa will rise again. The return of the Jedi.... lol lol lol...love and light---sufi

74

786...888... My love for our beloved cheikh Serigne Saliou is infinite; it defies the laws of gravity, like a rope that extends beyond the universe to spiritual planes, inhabited by unseen beings. Serigne Saliou is the ALL SEEING. Words cannot express that which exists beyond thought. Trade one life for another life that is false. Trade false reality for the Real. A continent full of the walking dead could not possibly help me obtain self-realization, so i moved to Touba. Escaping the idea of self is not easy. The ego is transparent, difficult to detect, we must all draw close to the cheikh to Reflect, introspect, and learn to neglect, the desires of the lowers self, burn like fire, crystallizing consciousness of the ONE, PRODUCING A DIMOND FROM CARBON. Sufism is death in the cheikh. One love-sufi

Read Surah Qiyamah

786... A close friend asked me if I had the desire to be 66.... This was my answer. i do not desire to be God. It is impossible for the wave to be the Ocean, but it is not impossible for the Ocean to be the wave!!! God is a secret inside the heart of every person, regardless of race or religion. When a person finds a way to purify his soul he/she becomes One with God. In fact we are never separate from God, just as a wave is never separate from the Ocean. Are sunray's separate from the sun? This is the relationship between the soul and God. The light of God was manifest to me some years ago, in a dream, when I was living with my cheikh in Africa. The Light appeared and the voice said, "I am a secret deep within your heart. Know Me and worship Me before you leave this earth. " The soul is a Ray of Light from God, hidden deep inside of the heart. When the soul is cleaned from the dirt of the world, the mind is purified from thoughts other than God, and the habits of conditioning have been broken, man manifests his innate Divinity.... Just as a seed that does not grow to become a flower in incomplete. A human being that does not manifest their hidden potential for Divinity is not complete...the soul is the seed potential of God, inside the heart. May we all find the water of Divinity to nourish this seed to fruition... love and light---sufi

76

786...A letter from Abdallah...The relationship between the cheikh or spiritual guide and his disciple is one of the more complex issues in the practical dimension of Sufism and can only be touched upon in the present context. All Sufis agree that entering the path without a cheikh is impossible. If someone thinks he has done so, in fact he has gone astray. The basic reason for the absolute necessity of the spiritual master is that the path is unknown before it is traversed, and a person cannot possibly prepare himself for the dangers and pitfalls that lurk on the way. The un-know ability of the path goes back to the un-know ability of God. That which can be known is that which He has taught us through revelation. Traveling the path is only possible through His guidance. Though the wide and easy path of the Shariat is incumbent upon all, the narrow and steep path of the Tariqat requires special qualifications on the part of the seeker and the person who shows the way. A second important reason for the necessity of the master is the principle set down in the Koranic verse, "Enter houses by their doors" (2:189). The door to knowledge of unseen things has been set up by God and His Prophet, and only the inheritors of the Prophet, designated by the silsilas or "chains of transmission" of the Sufi orders, are qualified to open those doors for others. Any attempt to enter this house by other than its door represents the utmost discourtesy toward God and His Prophet. Touba...love and light---sufi

77

786...Om tat va sat.... Brahman is All. The Self is Brahman. When Brahman is seated in the lotus of the heart, Brahman is known as the Atman, Self. This Self is Brahman, thus the self is All. The self is luminous beyond the veils of duality. The self is unborn ETERNAL, not effected by the passage of time, or any of the illusions related to the mind and the five senses. There is a teaching known as non-dual Advaita philosophy. Anyone on the path of self knowledge and Realization, should take a look at this non dual philosophy.... love and light---sufi, the self is ALL

78

786...The way of the sufi is transcends religion. It is the way of the heart. The way of Love. Sufism is an ancient tradition that is past down from master to student. It cannot be learned from books. Much of the path is subtle. It can only be received by transmission from the living master/cheikh/teacher. If you are interested in going on the sufi path feel free to visit us at our sufi school in Philly. The sufis say: if you stay in the rose garden, one day Hu will smell like a rose. Love and light - sufi

79

786.... Sufism is the true esoteric science of self Realization. It was taught in the pyramids of ancient Egypt. It was taught in the mountains of India. It was taught in Moorish Spain. It was taught by the 7 immortals in Asia. At one time in history, sufism was a practice without a name. Now it is a name without a practice. Sufism is the foundation of all esoteric schools. It teaches the true alchemy of the soul, the science of changing base metals (lower human qualities) to gold (Divine attributes). The 99 names (powers) all Allah exist in man in seed form, dormant, on the plane of the soul. The sufi science and practice gives the water of Light to these seeds of Divinity until they grow into fruition. Man/woman is not who he/she thinks they are.... We are all Eternal Beings of Light, knowing no birth and no death, but we grew up under the false chains of the slavery of false teachings about the Self, the Universe and Allah.... Can u imagine Hu you are looking at in the Mirror??? love and light---sufi

80

786... We thank Allah for satan, and the test and trials that he brings us. For without these test and trails we would not have become a wali (saint)"-sufi

The Beloved Prophet Muhammad (peace be upon him) has said, "The prophets have the highest tests and trails." The believers test and trails are given to them according to their level of Iman (faith). When I first started on this path (tariqat) an older disciple of my cheikh from Senegal said to me "Abdallah, I want the hardest test and trail possible." When I asked him why he wanted the hardest trials he smiled and said " the harder the trial, the higher the realization." In or way, the harder the test and trails you receive the higher your Self Realization will be. It is the high pressure that causes the crystallization of carbon to a diamond. This "internal combustion" that the disciple goes through during test and trails causes the alchemical change to take place on the level of the soul, causes the alchemical change to take place on the level of the soul. Without this change on the level of the soul, there can be no spiritual growth...if you are not being tested with trials you should ask your self, am I on the true path? Allah says in the Quran that He "test those who try to come close to him."... love and light---sufi

81

786... Cheikh Abdul-Qadir al-Jilani said: "At the first stage one recites the name of God with one's tongue; then when the heart becomes alive one recites inwardly. At the beginning one should declare in words what one remembers. Then stage by stage the remembrance spreads throughout one's being -- descending to the heart then rising to the soul; then still further it reaches the realm of the secrets; further to the hidden; to the most hidden of the hidden."" one love-sufi

82

786...Traveling through the illusion of life at the speed of GOD, we came upon the illusion of the lower self. The lower self is worse than 70 shaytan on the outside. It is one of the 4 enemies we must defeat on the journey to Self Realization/Divine Proximity. The lower self can be defeated with the techniques given by a living master. One of the weapons used to defeat the lower self is fasting. The lower self is similar to an angry animal that is ready to strike. If the animal is not given food for a few days, it would normally lose the strength and desire to fight. This is the same with the lower self. Over eating causes the heart to grow hard.

Fasting weakens the strength of the lower self, making our acts of worship and meditation more effective. A decrease in this world often results in an increase in the spiritual world. My master, Cheikh Ahmadou Bamba, has said, "the sufi eats less, talks less, and sleeps less." A true living master is needed to learn the science of internal alchemy, turning the lower base qualities into Divine attributes.... love and light---sufi

83

786...The Self is Luminous. If you do not see Allah and know Allah within your Self, you will never see and know Allah. Today i was at the Bawa Muhaiyadeen Fellowship in Philly. i had a deep deep deep conversation with Cheikh Muhaiyadeen in the meeting room. His talk is always on the level of haqiqat and marifat. At the end of the talk with me i went into a transcendental state and screamed "Allah" in a very loud voice. i got up and walked out on the room saying, Allah, Allah, Allah.... What he said to me cannot be repeated here... Just know that we are all living in a dream world far from the Divine reality. Our lives have become stages for illusion, false hood, and the race for hell and lower desires. If we do not wake up before we are woke up, it will be the end of a long long dream that was only dust in the wind. i am begging all of my readers to do as i did. Find a living master, and sit at his or her feet until you experience death before death. Please, please, please try to find a living master who can breath the spark of Divinity directly into your soul, and wake up from the nightmare illusion dream that you call your life...love and light---sufi

84

786...wa laikum as salam...sufism is an ocean, only the sincere seeker should seek the pearl at the bottom of the ocean. You have asked some good questions. Sufism is the esoteric science of Self-realization in the Islamic context. Sufism is the science of removing the illusionary separation between man and God. The journey of the sufi cannot be told in words, the journey takes place in the heart. The sufi has the true science of soul purification. There are 7 levels of the nafs (soul). When the seven levels have been purified a marriage between the soul and the spirit takes place. When this mystical union has been reached, man and Allah are one. Allah has said " i become the eyes he sees with, the ears he hears with, the mouth he speaks with, the hands he grasps with, the feet he walks with." in the Holy Quran Allah has said "he indeed succeeds who purifies it." the sufis have said that "it" refers to the soul/heart...love and light---sufi

85

786.... Oh wise Sufi saint, how can a loving relationship between a man and woman be comparable to that of the love of the divine and is it possible that a love relationship like that can benefit all existence? That's funny, you talking to me? You have asked an important question man and woman are symbols of the duality that is found in the principle of the Divine. Man and woman are outward manifestations of the polarization of the Divine Light that is transcendent, beyond the planes of duality. Allah says in the Quran "I created creation in pairs." when man and woman join together, through the union of Love, this represent Allah, knowing Himself, through the union of opposites. The sufis have said, Allah is known through His opposites. Allah is the First, Last, Hidden, Manifest, Giver of Live, Bringer of Death. What appear to be opposites are in fact ONE Reality. This reality, when seen from the viewpoint of the mind has duality. In Reality this One Being can only Be ONE. When man and woman UNITE, this is the secret of tantra, the union of the male and female principle to form the DIVINE...this can benefit all existence because each person is a complete manifestation of the ALL...love and light, the one you love, love you i...sufi

86

786... When the student is ready, the teacher/friend will appear... All of us on this path of sufism are one family of light. We need each other on this path. Sometimes we refer to it as the spiritual support group. Some experiences i have had on this path would make the average person sell everything and move under a bridge. Without other spiritual travelers to share our experiences with, the path would not be the same. An old sufi saying goes "grapes grow ripe on the vine together." the shaytan/devil only attacks the lone sheep. One of the most dangerous ways shaytan attacks us is through our own mind with negative thoughts, and doubts about reality. The Illustrious Buddha has said, "99% of our problems are in the mind."...You should find a good friend to share your experiences with...it has been said that we have big ears...they are open if you want to share.... as salam alaikum.... love and light----sufi

87

786... Dear seeker of Light, Life is short... We will never know the reason why we crossed paths on our journey back to God/Self. Be sure that you are a Divine Being. You are not the physical body. You are a ray of Gods Light inhabiting a human body. You may never experience your true identity because of the mind and the illusion of this world of false duality. All is ONE. You are my true Self manifest in a different form. i don't know you and we may never meet on this plane. Be sure that when you leave your body you will know the truth of reality. Try to find a way to awaken from the deep sleep of false identity of self...love and light----sufi 88

A friend has asked me a few good questions....

Tell me where are you from. What is your heritage, your age, and what is it that your hope to accomplish while here on earth? (If you don't mind answering :)

786.... i am from Allah. My heritage is Divine. My age is eternal.... i hope to know, worship and return to Oneness with Allah while here on earth and help others do the same...love and light---sufi

89

787... Trapped inside of lower self, we decided to find an exit from the matrix. The path was covered with dirt and rubbish; it was not detectable to the naked eye, until my master removed the seals from my eyes, ears and heart. The not in my tongue has been untied by the Light of the Divine. Allah is All and the Self is that. Walking between the two worlds requires extreme balance and patience with those who think they are only mortal. We are all Divine but the passage through the birth canal causes complete memory loss that results in temporary insanity until we meet with the Divine on this plane of duality and illusion. The physical body is the clothes worn by the ETERNAL BEING OF LIGHT that you are. Do not be confused by the lies of the living dead. God, Allah, Brahman, is not other than the TRUE SELF... Try to remember HU U R.... and wake up from the deep sleep of forgetfulness... Today i did not feel like watering the teachings down. God is having a human experience, and She is waiting for you to die, so He can take over.... love and light----sufi

90

786... The test of Allah are for those who He Loves. The Prophet Muhammad has said (alay he salam) that the prophets are tested the most by Allah. Allah says in the Quran that He test those who try to come close to Him. Allah never abandons us. It is said that when we feel close to Allah we are far from Him, and when we feel far from Allah we are close to Allah. Look for the blessing to come from Allah when we are in the trials of life, not when the wind is blowing at our backs and everything is going good. You can be sure that you are with Allah. Do not feel like Allah has abandoned you. Allah says that He is closer to us than are jugular vein, and Allah also says in the Quran when they ask about Me; tell them that I am near. Dear seeker, we are praying for your internal peace and well-being. You should start to say this verse from the Quran as a zikr; it will help you in your time of trials and bring you heart to a state of peace. The verse is: La ee la ha ill la anta. Sub ha na ka ee nee koon toom me nal ah thal lee meen. ----English: there is none worthy of worship but You (Allah), glory be unto you. Surely i am of those who have wronged themselves... please use this verse at least 129x once during the day and once during the night. This will work for you. There is a secret in this verse that cannot be discussed on the internet. Please keep in touch with me. You have a good heart. Allah loves you and is helping you!!!! Love and light---sufi

91

786...."When you give your adoration to a great being what you are really celebrating is your own higher Self, your own greater Consciousness. When you give your love to an exalted one, you feel so uplifted that at least for a few brief moments, you are in seventh heaven; you are living in the sahasrara, the highest spiritual center in the crown of the head, with the awareness of So'ham: I am that. Out of their love for the people of this earth, the great beings take form and live among us. If you catch even a tiny glimpse of how much love they have for people, for animals and everything that is worthy of love, then your heart soars with delight. You are filled with conviction. You know that by being in their presence and following their teachings, you are walking the right path. To inhale the fragrance of the teachings of the masters, to be embraced by their wisdom, to receive their blessings, to have the courage to discover a new day every morning". ----by Gurumani

Ya Muhammad sala alayka 1000x a day is Tarbiya for the soul.

786... Ya Rasool lu la. Ya Habib ul la. Ya Mustapha. Allah hu ma sali ala say dee na Muhammad, al fati he lee ma oog lee ka, wal ka tee me le ma sa ba ka, nasi reel haqqi bill haqqi wal hadi, ee la see ra te kal moos ta keem. Wa ala ali he, haqq kad kad ree he, wal mik dar re hill ahteem!!!!!

..."He who knows himself, knows his Lord."-Prophet Muhammad peace bee upon him eternally.... in essence our beloved Prophet Muhammad has said she who knows herself knows Allah. If knowing the self is knowing Allah then i ask the question "what is the self?" i recently shared with a dear friend of mine on the path the aphorism "in ignorance Brahman and the self are thought to be two. In Light they are known to be ONE." the true Self is not different from Allah. In fact Allah is the unseen essence of all things in existence. Once my cheikh said to me when i was living with him in Senegal "if you see something and do not see Allah manifest through it, know that your understanding of the Tawheed (Oneness) of Allah is limited." In the west, unless you grew up in a syda yoga ashram (smile Q) we are taught false ideas about the self. Thus there is a need for a journey to self. When we journey back to true self, we have to leave behind all of the false ideas about the self that we were indoctrinated with by society. Just as a snake sheds its skin, and continues living we must find away to release these false ideas about self and live in the reality of Oneness with Allah, the true SELF...Ramadan Mubarak.... 6:25am just after fajr salat.... love and light sufi

93

I have A LOT of questions. I am anxious to learn and understand so if you wouldn't mind sharing your knowledge I would be grateful. As I mentioned the only two religions / philosophies I have been exposed to are Christianity and Buddhism. Does the Quran (forgive any spelling mistakes) pre-date the bible? Are there any links between Christianity and Muslim religions? I have heard a lot of different things but I am not sure what is true and what is someone's guess.

786... The Quran and the Bible are chapters from one book known as the Mother of the Books. In fact all of the true holy books are chapters from this ONE book that exists with Allah/God. Any differences in the holy books are from man and not from God. The Old testament and the Quran agree on just about 90%. The old testament and the new testament are very different and do not agree on many things. There is only a small difference between the Old testament and the Quran. All of the major prophets in the Bible are mentioned in the Quran and their stories are even explained in more detail in the Quran. Example: in the Quran Allah explains the virgin birth of Jesus and how the Angel Gabriel came to here in the form of a well made man to announce the virgin birth.... there is much mooooore that could be said on this topic but i hope this is enough for now. love and light ---sufi 94

786.... al hum do li la, the answers to your questions would make a good book on tassawuf/sufism...some Muslims turn Islam into a business deal. They feel like just because they worship Allah He has to pay them with Jannah. Their worship is not true worship; they only worship for a reward, not because Allah, in His Beauty and Majesty is worthy of worship. The 7 stations of the soul can bee found in the Holy Quran: 1. Animal soul 2. Self-accusing soul 3. Soul inspired to do good 4. Soul at peace 5. Soul well pleased with Allah

6. Soul Allah is well pleased with 7. Perfected soul. There is a book called Degrees of the Soul that explains these 7 levels in detail, most books on the soul only go over the first 4 levels. Most people only make it to the second level because it is at this level that we begin to blame ourselves for the negative actions that we do. If we stop doing these negative actions and become inspired to do good then we have reached the third level, but for a person without a cheikh this is very rare. It is impossible to reach the fourth through the seventh level without the guidance of a cheikh. Haqiqat means knowing the Truth of Reality, and Marifat means knowing Allah. There is only a small difference between the two. A true Living cheikh is one who has completed the journey, and has the permission of Allah and the Prophet to guide others on the path. Yes it is possible to follow a cheikh in another country. My cheikh is in Touba Senegal, and i am in America, at the beginning of the journey it is best to be in the same country with the cheikh, but when the internal connection is firm, the True cheikh will be with you wherever you are on the planet. We pray that these answers are suitable. Feel free to ask more if you need to. as salam alaikum, love and light-sufi

95

786.... My dear friend, i too am a scientist. i study the science of Self. Of all things we can know the Self is the greatest. Our beloved Prophet Muhammad has said, "she who knows herself, knows Allah." Islam is not a religion; it is a way of life that has the power to first establish the soul in a state of internal peace. From that internal peace we are able to reach Divine proximity and ultimately realize that only Allah is real, and the universe is an Illusion that only exists in the mind. A rope may be mistaken for a snake. When we realize it is only a rope, we know that the snake never existed. Thus upon awakening from the deep sleep in the false self, man will realize that the universe never existed and that God is the only REALITY.... Islam is a science that wakes man up from his or her sleep in the false self. You speak of levitation, healing and other miracles. All of these things are possible for the true realized human Being. We hope this helps you on your way. Feel free to ask any questions...love and light---sufi

96

786... You are on the edge of the mountain... This path goes in cycles; i have been to that point several times. The last time it happened to me i left everything and went to live in Senegal with my master for two years.... When the call of Light comes there is nothing we can do to suppress it. Be careful, and walk slowly on the edge of the mountain. We are indeed strangers in this world of illusion traveling back to self. This call will continue to come until you reach a certain level of balance in your spiritual practice. Walking in the spiritual world can be dangerous if we do not have balance. Some mystics experience kundalini like you expressed and never make it back to this side of reality. Some become trapped between the two worlds and you see them, communicating with spirits we cannot see, talking to themselves on park benches or walking around picking up trash all day. Remember in the Bhagavad-Gita Lord Krishna has said "the highest yogi is not the one in the cave dreaming about the city, it is the yogi in the city dreaming about the cave." my advice to you is keep your job and try to find a point of non-attachment to the job. Become the neutral observer of the movie of life who is not effected by the changing scenes in the movie...if this does not work, you can always say fuck it, move to Philly and live in our sufi school...SMILE...love and light---sufi

97

786... intoxicated

desire is the root cause of all suffering knowing this i still long for your presence intoxicated by the very thought of you your essence is Divine Being of Light manifesting positive shakti this feeling could easily be mistaken for Bhakti union of the opposites beyond all forms of duality you are me, i am you one Divine Being existing, manifesting as two.... inspired by U.....love and light----- sufi

98

786... Please tell me about the true self, the real I? OM TAT VA SAT... The true self is the eternal true self of ALL. i am a Divine Being of Light having a human experience in order to know my self. i created this universe and exist as the very fabric of all existence. The true self is ALL. Knowing no birth and no death, i am the eternal i, existing in a state of oneness with Divinity, i am beyond duality and the pairs of opposites, knowing no illusion of separateness from the Divine. My true self is the lover and the Beloved.... Does this answer your question??? love and light---sufi

99

786... Sufis study (ilm ul huroof) the science of numbers and letters. In this science the Arabic letters are given numerical values. Prayers can be turned into numbers. 786 is the numerical value for the Arabic prayer: BIS ME LA IR RAHMAN IR RAHEEM: which means: IN THE NAME OF GOD THE BENIFICIENT THE MERCIFULL. This prayer has many benefits, to many to list in fact. It should be used at the start of every endeavor. Saying this prayer 313x can ward off enemies and negative energy. 21x before going to sleep is also a BIG SECRET... This prayer, if used in a specific way with a specific number can be used to bring things to the disciple.... This prayer also has the power to protect you from jinns if you use it while being in a state of ritual purity. The sufi has the science of invocation of the Divine. Each of the 99 names of Allah has a specific numerical value that goes with it. Let me stop here, some things are not to be played with...love and light---sufi

Sri Shirdi Sai Baba Namaha!!!

786... Om Sai Baba Om.... transcendental Love of the Divine, moves kundalini up my spine. intoxicated by celestial wine, i go inside my Self to find... I Am That...OM TAT VA SAT... love and light---sufi

101

786... We have had the same question for years. In the Quran Allah very rarely uses the pronoun i for Himself, Allah very often says we. Example: 'We created the heavens and the earth.' Sometimes 'i' use the pronoun 'we' in the same way, about myself. The only problem is when we do it in conversation like 'we are going to the store' people always ask, who else is going???? Try this and see how it works for 'you'...love and light...sufi

102

786.... Tears for the shadow less prophet... This is for the lovers... If i shed 1 million tears for 1 million years, it would not be enough to show my love for the shadow less prophet, the light of both worlds, the shifa for the sinner, the reason for creation, the entire universe was created because of the shadow less prophet, our Beloved Habib, SAYDINA MUHAMMAD, the best of all creation, Being of light, bringing the light to those seeking the light, the prophet of light, guide to the light, revealer of the light, from the light, in the light, the reality of the LIGHT, how could you ever have a shadow??????? May eternal blessings and peace be upon you Oh Mustapha Nabi, Muhammad until the Day of Judgment and beyond...love eternal to you...sufi

103

786.... as salam alaikum.... i was once told that sufism is a strict application of the shariat, with a different intention. The intention of the sufi is Divine Proximity. My cheikh, Cheikh Ahmadou Bamba has said, "If it is not in the Quran or the Sunnah, it is not from me." Sufism is the third part of our deen that no one talks about. Our deen is Iman, Islam, and Ihsan. Sufism is Ihsan. True sufism comes from our Beloved Prophet Muhammad peace be upon him.

The sufi path is the path of love. This path must be learned from one who has completed the path, the living teacher/cheikh. If you are Blessed to find a true living sufi master as a guide, you have found the best gift that life can give. May Allah bless you in your search and journey...feel free to ask any question...love and light----sufi

104

786... Do you know who you are? There is more to man/woman than meets the eye... if you think that you "know" yourself because you know your physical qualities, name, age, race, gender and birthday, then you have a loooooong way to go to knowledge of self. My cheikh once said to me that people take initiation with him for something that the naked eye cannot see or detect. What was he talking about?

You are not the you that you have come to know...the "you" that you know is the false you, based totally on ILLUSION~~ you are in a state of emergency, and the worst part is you do not even know it. Living in a false reality, leads to false hopes and dreams, and by the time you wake up, it will be to late...find a way to "Know Thy

Self." the Self is an Eternal Light having a human experience...in Knowing this Self you will "wake up from the deep sleep of unknowing" and live beyond the pair of opposites that we call duality...love and light---sufi

105

786... Memories of the future bring back visions of the past existing in the ever present now the unseen has become seen prophets, angels and ethereal beings appear in my awakened dreams a window opened between worlds when the sun crossed the horizon of consciousness existing in an extreme state of bliss oneness is all that exist ONENESS beyond the individual "i" lies a wide open sky were there is no "u" and "i" transcendental experiences with the Divine caused by long periods of internal alchemy removed subconscious lines of separation resulted in crystallization of Being freeing the soul from the bondages of time and space memories of the future.......love and light----sufi

106

The Heart Sutra Body is nothing more than emptiness, emptiness is nothing more than body. The body is exactly empty, and emptiness is exactly body. The other four aspects of human existence -- feeling, thought, will, and consciousness -- are likewise nothing more than emptiness, and emptiness nothing more than they.

All things are empty: Nothing is born, nothing dies, nothing is pure, nothing is stained, nothing increases and nothing decreases. So, in emptiness, there is no body, no feeling, no thought, no will, no consciousness. There are no eyes, no ears, no nose, no tongue, no body, no mind. There is no seeing, no hearing, no smelling, no tasting, no touching, no imagining. There is nothing seen, nor heard, nor smelled, nor tasted, nor touched, nor imagined. There is no ignorance, and no end to ignorance. There is no old age and death, and no end to old age and death. There is no suffering, no cause of suffering, no end to suffering, no path to follow. There is no attainment of wisdom, and no wisdom to attain. The Bodhisattvas rely on the Perfection of Wisdom, and so with no delusions, they feel no fear, and have Nirvana here and now. All the Buddha's, past, present, and future, rely on the Perfection of Wisdom, and live in full enlightenment. The Perfection of Wisdom is the greatest mantra. It is the clearest mantra, the highest mantra, the mantra that removes all suffering. This is truth that cannot be doubted. Say it so: Gaté, gaté, paragaté, parasamgaté. Bodhi! Swara!

Which means... Gone, gone, gone beyond, gone beyond gone. Hail to the goer!!!!!

107

786.... Light returns to Light. Energy is neither created nor destroyed. We are not the human beings that we believe are selves to be. The idea's we accept about self from society are totally false. The true self has no race, religion, birth or death. True self is eternal. We are all eternal beings of Light having a hu-man experience in the school on contrast and duality in order to return to the Light, our true self. Just for the record Hu is an ancient Arabic name for God. So by definition the human, hu-man-being, is God existing in the form of man. Sadly enough because of the darkness of illusion, and earthly desires that cover the heart, man has descended to a level below that of the animals. Find a way to purify the heart. One way is by chanting the heart sutra: gatay, gatay, para gatay, para som gatay, Bodhi swara."---"Gone, gone, gone beyond, gone beyond gone, hail to the goer!!!!!"----love and light---sufi, the self of your self

108

786.... Approaching Divinity Becoming transparent, I manifest divinity me, myself, and I, Form the Holy Trinity in oneness, my essence knows no multiplicity. The vibration of light slowed down creates matter. Meditation stills the chatter of the mind. The first rung of the ladder, of self-realization is hard to find. It lies at the base of the spine; I have been in heaven several times. When the serpent starts to climb I am intoxicated by celestial wine. Engulfed by the light, in reality I do not exist. The lover dies in the love of the fire of the beloved's kiss. I am that I am. I am approaching divinity. 18,000 universes exist inside of me. The self of the self can only be measured by infinity. Definitely, definitively I am approaching divinity. Seeing myself beyond the body on the astral plane of the soul was completely perplexing. Etheric light body kissed by 3 immortal fish, from the see of darkness 4 gates in the heavens opened. Some things are not to be spoken. Extreme states of bliss preceded gnosis disappearing in oneness from the closeness-Becoming transparent, I manifest divinity me, myself, and I form the Holy Trinity, in oneness. My essence knows no multiplicity. The vibration of light slowed down made me. – Sufi

109

786.... Mysticism is the unfolding of the spirit as a flower is hidden in the bud, when the bud unfolds, there is the flower and the fragrance; likewise when the spirit unfolds there appears beauty and grace in life.

-Hakim Tirmidi

110

786... love love love!!!! i do not know you but i bet you are experiencing some form of a feeling of a lack of love... My friend, whatever you are going through be sure that Allah Loves you and is with you...YOU MUST FOCUS ON ALLAH AND NOT YOUR PROBLEMS. The world is full of problems. To be honest most people are full of shit, and will let you down if given the chance. The wise person learns to focus on Allah in the midst of any depression, or negative situation. This way the problems of the world do not effect/hurt us. i do not know what you are going through, but suicide is not the answer..... The saint is the sinner who got up one more time than they fell down.... Tell shaytan/the devil to stop whispering into you ear. Thoughts of suicide are from the devil, they are not from the self.... May Allah give you the strength to fight the whisperings of the shaytan, and remain in a state of eternal Salam (peace).... love and light---sufi

111

786... Very good answers. Try to find out more about the three Gunas, they are important. They also relate to three main character types, and can be used as a map on the journey to Self. The Gita teaches that the highest yogi is the one in the city working who is focused on the Divine, and not the yogi in the cave who is thinking about the city.

Work in the world, without attachment to the fruit of action, is one of the fastest ways to Self Realization...

How can i "reach union with Brahman"? You are Brahman; you must find a way to remove the Doubts of the mind, and thoughts of duality and separation. If you ever have what i call "the God experience" you will know beyond the shadow of a doubt your true Reality. Until this happens it will only be philosophy...

love and light----sufi

Recite Surah Iklas 200x/day for Tasfiya of the soul

786...as salam alaikum... You have asked an important question, "what should we ask Allah for?" It is said, "sometimes when Allah wants to punish us, He gives us what we ask for." The best thing to ask Allah for is "Allah." This is a high concept. We ask Allah for Allah. There are two verses in the Quran that can take care of our needs. These two verses are the last two verses of the second chapter of the Holy Quran. Once when i was in northern Senegal, just across the river from Mauritania, i asked the tijani cheikh there for some advice on my path. He told me "read the last two verses of the second chapter as often as possible, they will help you." the prophet Muhammad has said in the hadith, there are two verses in the Quran that will take care of your needs. When they asked what the verses were, he said "the last two verses of the second chapter." Cheikh Nazim has said that there are some station with Allah that you will not reach if you are not reading these two verses...love and light----sufi

113

786.... Ask your self the question "who am i?" if you answer with anything related to name, race, sex, time, or place, then you have no idea who/Hu u r!!! You are not the "you" that you have come to know. You only know the false you that you have been living with. Your desires, wants, likes, and dislikes are all from the "imaginary you." from your past experiences you have created a type of "actor" on an imaginary stage, that you call life. This "you" is a total ILLUSION, that lives in your own dream world...dreams are for those who are sleep. i am praying that you wake up from your state of self hypnosis, and try to find the true YOU, that is HU...you are a Divine Being trapped in the false idea of what you call "you." have a good-**days** sleep, and i hope that "you" wake up before you are woke up....love and light---sufi

114

The Roots of Misfortune and Loss

Abu'l Hassan ash-Shadhili, may Allah be pleased with him, said, "My beloved once gave me council. He said, 'Do not move your feet except wherever you hope for the reward of Allah. Do not sit except in a place where you are completely secure from the disobedience of Allah. Do not keep company except with one who can assist you in the obedience of Allah. And realize that they are few.'" He also said, may Allah be pleased with him, "Whoever directs you towards this world has deceived you. Whoever directs you towards work has burdened you. Whoever directs you to Allah, has given you sound advice." He also said, "Make fearful awareness (*taqwa*) your country, then the praise of people will not harm you. This is as long as you do not become satisfied with your errors, persist in sins, or as long as your fear of Allah does not cease when you are alone." I say, that the above three are the foundations of misfortune and loss (*usuul 'l-balaayaa wa 'l-afaat*).

115

786... Up and down, up and down, you need to find balance in your life. Any problem that you have is small in God's eyes. You have a house, health, sanity, family, shoes and countless other blessings that outweigh any negativity that you have in your life... didn't you wake up this mourning? Just think about all the people that died last night, and all of the people that woke up without true knowledge of Self and God... to me, not having knowledge of Self, is like living in hell because: not knowing self, means not knowing God, not knowing God means living in hell. Try to count the blessings of Allah in your life, and do not focus on the small negatives. "The woman with no shoes prays to Allah for shoes until she see's the woman with no feet." love and light---sufi

116

786... Dear traveler on the path of Truth, you have asked about our Beloved Prophet Muhammad, peace and blessings be upon him. He is the first and the last prophet sent to mankind. In the Quran it says he was sent as a Mercy to all of the universes!!! He said "i was a prophet when Adam was between clay and water." The only people to have some clue about the reality of Muhammad are the sufis. Prophet Muhammad was a man of Light. He did not have a shadow. When he traveled across the desert as a youth, clouds would follow him to protect him from the heat of the sun. When he was a child, two angels came to him, took out his heart, and washed it clean with waters from heaven. As an adult he was an acetic. Before the angel Gabriel came to him at the age of forty, the prophet used to meditate in a cave every year for 40 days. He was known as Al-Amin (the truthful) by the people in Mecca, and he never worshiped the gods and idols of the Kabba. He always believed in the ONE God. Once during his prophet hood, he split the moon in half for those who wanted to test him. If you ever read the Quran you will know that he is a prophet. The knowledge in the Quran could not have come from a man. In the Quran it talks about the development of the fetus in the womb, and it even talks about the barrier in the ocean between the salt and the fresh water. These are two things that man did not have knowledge of when the Quran was revealed. The prophet Muhammad is the master, and guide of the sufi on the path to Realization. He is still seen today by many of us in visions and while in the wake state. We hope that this helps you to understand a little more about ore Beloved prophet Muhammad peace and blessings be upon him. love and light--- sufi

117

PURIFICATION OF THE HEART AND THE MEMBERS OF THE BODY

By Cheikh Ahmadou Bamba

The Heart is like the image of the king among the members of the body; anywhere that the body goes, the other members are supported with Mercy (under its influence)

So, you should want to improve the whole body and all of its members for the FACE of the ONE that subjugated His enemies

Purify your Heart of dull spots until it is in Intimacy with ALLAH

Those that perceive beyond a thing, other that ALLAH, the SINGLE ONE, are Apostate. Anyone that is not rebellious toward ALLAH will foresee Him in everything and ALLAH will grant them excellent gifts in what they see

[You should] purify your Heart from defects and avoid them with the best of virtues

Avoid jealousy, ostentation, pride, hatred, so that you may draw perspicacity from them

As for ostentation, it is a minor sin of association; those that are sullied with such a vice will be eternally deposed

Neither science, nor action are profitable with ostentation, those that are imbued with these join together all misfortunes

Naturally [you should] direct yourself towards the LORD OF POWER, in all verbal expressions (words) and actions (deeds)

The way of purifying the Heart is long; those that are engaged in this must place their confidence in ALLAH, the SUBLIME ONE

The lazy cannot comprehend how sins affect an individual!

- Cheikh Ahmadou Bamba

118

Who is the cheikh dressed in all white?

786... The cheikh in my picture dressed in all white is Cheikh Ahmadou Bamba, the founder of the Murid Sufi Order, and the Holy city of Touba in Senegal west Africa. Cheikh Ahmadou Bamba is one of the greatest sufi masters to ever walk this earth. Many pictures of him were taken, and he would never show up in the picture. The family members asked him to let them take a picture, and begged him to "show up" this time. That is why there is only one picture of him!

Cheikh Ahmadou Bamba lived less than 100 years ago. He left this world in 1927. He was visited by our Beloved Prophet Muhammad (peace be upon him) many times in the waking state. He was a master of many sufi orders, including the Qadaria, Shadalia, and Tijani. In his lifetime he was also visited by the other Sufi masters of his time from Morocco, Mauritania, Mecca, Medina, and many other countries.

The French colonialist exiled Cheikh Ahmadou Bamba two times for a total of 10 years. They tried to kill the sheikh many times, and by many different means, such as poison, and fire. They even tried to shoot the cheikh with a firing squad, but they could not kill him. On one occasion Cheikh Ahmadou Bamba walked on water and made salat on the ocean because the French told him he could not pray on the boat they were taking him to exile on. Many books have been written about him in French, Arabic and English, and he is still one of the best-kept secrets in the history of Africa, Islam and Sufism. The Magal is the celebration/commemoration of his exile by the French from Senegal to Gabon. The Magal is celebrated world wide, and in every major city in America, on the 18th of Safar on the lunar calendar. Insha Allah. The event is free, and everyone is invited. The event will include Sufi chanting of the cheikhs poetry, Quran recitation, speeches, and Senegalese dinner.

Love and Light---sufi

119

786... Sufism is feeding people-high sufi wisdom In Senegal west Africa; my beloved cheikh feeds more than 1000 people every Saturday. Every Wednesday, he feeds over 500 students in the Quran school (Darrah). On the average, about 100 people a day, eat at his house. I saw all of this with my own eyes when I was living with him. Sufism is feeding people. I am asking all of the people that I can to feed at least one homeless person a month. Some friends and me have decided to do this on the last Saturday of every month in Philadelphia. I would like to see how many "friends" I can get to do the same thing in their location. All you have to do is cook some food, even if it is only enough for one person, and give it away. It is that simple. Allah/God will bless you for this act...please let me now if you would like to join us in this small effort. Once a disciple asked Cheikh Ibra Fall "even though I don't pray and fast a lot, what can I do to have the high station of the saints before me?" Cheikh Ibra Fall told the man "cook food and give it away, this will give you the high station of the saints before you." thank you in advance... Love and Light---sufi

Cheikh and Disciple

The term "companionship" *(suhba)* is a general designation for the disciple's relationship to the cheikh. There is companionship in the specific sense of undergoing training at the hands of a master, and in the more general sense of visiting the master and acquiring his blessing.

To revere the cheikh is to show reverence for none but God, so revere him out of courtesy toward God in God.

The cheiks are the courteous, and proximity aids them in guiding and strengthening in God

They are the inheritors of all the messengers, so their words come only from God.

You see them like the prophets among their enemies, never asking from God anything but God.

But if a state should appear in them which distracts them from the Shariat, leave them with God-

Follow not after them and walk not in their tracks, for they are God's freedmen in God.

Be not guided by him from whom the Shariat has gone, even if he brings news from God!

When we saw that nowadays the disciples are ignorant of the levels of their cheiks, we said concerning that:

Ignored are the measures of the cheiks, the people of witnessing and firm rooting!

People consider their words low out of ignorance, though they stand in a lofty degree!

The cheiks are deputies of the Real in the cosmos, like the messengers in their time. Rather, the cheiks are the inheritors, those who have inherited the knowledge of the revealed Laws from the prophets, though the cheiks do not set down the Law. It belongs to them to preserve the Shariat for everyone; it is not theirs to make the Law. It belongs to them to help the elect preserve their hearts and observe the rules of courtesy. [The Sufi Path of Knowledge] – Ibn Arabi

121

786... This is an email i got today from a disciple of my cheikh... i wanted to share it with my FRIENDS...enjoy...

The family tree of the human race goes back to the One Source. Allah says in the Quran that after the completion of Adam's creation from clay, Allah breathed into him of His Spirit and that is how man came to be. "Min Ruhihi", of My Spirit and therefore we became related or linked to the Source of our creation. We are not Him and yet we are not separate from Him. In Sufism we learn the concept of ¡Huwa/La Huwa" from the detailed expositions of mystical philosophy by masters such as Ibn al Arabi. "Huwa/La Huwa" means He/Not He. The great master says that the whole of creation balances on the words ¡Huwa/La Huwa". In our distance from Him and in His transcendence we are far removed from Him. By virtue of "min ruhihi" and having been created in "His Image" we reflect His Being. The "deen" or debt that we owe Allah is to surrender that part of His back to Him. The Quran testifies to the ultimate human victory as being the successful purification of the soul. The soul or "nafs" that has been purified of the confusion and erroneous belief stemming from the apparent multiplicity has attained eternal felicity (Touba). This is Islam, when we have paid our debt to Allah in the form of unconditional surrender (Jebelu/Bayat).

(((888)))

122

Advice from the Guru The goal of life is liberation from all the troubles of life. If we get everything in life, but fail to get liberation, then it means that we have not finished our duty in this life. There are four goals in the life of everyone. They are dharma (religious duties), artha (wealth), kama (fulfillment of desires) and moksha (liberation). Everyone wants money and enjoyment, but without righteousness, they are dangerous. They will lead a person to live like a demon. There must be righteousness with money and desires. With righteous living one reaches the last goal of moksha (liberation). It is better to have salvation during one's life (jivan mukti). Kabir Saheb said that if you cannot obtain salvation in life, how could you obtain it in death? Who can bear witness that someone got salvation after death? Salvation is worthwhile only if it is realized in one's life. This salvation is obtained through devotion, meditation and attunement with the Divine Word inside.

123

786... 7 levels, purification of the soul

Sufism is an ocean. There is much more to learn... the journey of the sufi takes place in the heart, on the plane of the soul/nafs... do you know the 7 levels of the soul/nafs? This is the next thing you should study. The 7 levels are the road map of the sufi. You must know were you are and were you are going. Purification of the 7 levels of the soul is the sufi way. Without tazkiyah-tul-nafs (purification of the soul) there is no Realization. The cheikh is the doctor of the soul. He/she has the medicine for the healing and purification...there are many different ways to purify the soul. When you learn the 7 levels, insha Allah we will start on this journey together.... love and light---sufi

786...Walking on this path...

Walking on this path sometimes is hectic

Uphill

Trials should be expected

Turn back

Turn back the hands of time

Mind over matter

Meditate to still the mind

Illusion

Clouds perception

Question

Am I in the right direction?

Death is a bridge that must be crossed

Study the map now so you won't be lost

The spirit plane

Vibrates faster

Kundalini should only be raised by a master

Life

Is a game similar to chess

Step

Away from the board

And you can see it best

Master

Tantra, mantra, duality, yin yang

Eastern philosophy

Sufi, I ching

Return of the

Tai chi jedi

Opening of the third eye

Die before you die

And become immortal

The Egyptian mysteries have been revealed

This is the turning of the seventh wheel

Hidden wisdom for the masses in Aquarius

Rise up sankofa

The phoenix shall fly again

We are experiencing total recall

Of higher planes of existence before the fall

The matrix is real

This is a holographic universe

The theory of relativity must be reversed

Light upon light

Experience the transmission

What will it take to raise our condition?

love and light----sufi

125

786... Life is a movie Once when I was sitting with my cheikh in Africa he said to the disciples "life is a dream." Life is a dream; do not be disturbed by the changing scenes in the movie. Whatever comes let it come from Allah. Whatever goes, let it go to Allah...our Beloved Prophet Muhammad (eternal peace and blessing be upon him), has said in the hadith "the pen is lifted, and the ink is dry." What does this mean? It means that Allah wrote everything that happens to us in this life before it happened. Events in our life are like scenes in a movie that were previously wrote in the script. In the Quran Allah says, "the good is from Allah, and the bad is from your own hands." One sufi once said to me; since life is a movie, try to play a good character in the movie!!! Everyone knows what happens to the bad guy at the end of the movie LOL... Love and Light---sufi

126

786... wisdom, courage, temperance, and justice

The foundation of good character

According to Imam Al-Ghazali

According to Imam Al Ghazali wisdom is "a condition of the soul by which we distinguish truth from falsehood in our actions." Courage is "the subjugation of impatience to the intellect." Temperance is "the controlling of the desires by the intellect and the Shariat (spiritual law)." Justice is "a power and condition in the soul by which we control the expansion and contraction of anger and lower desires by wisdom."

Imam Ghazali (may Allah be well pleased with him) has said, " it is by the equilibrium of these 4 principles that all good character proceed."

Our Beloved Prophet Muhammad, sulk la hu alay he wa salam, has said, " I came to perfect good character." Sufism is the way that leads to the perfection of good character. By following the way of the beloved prophet, and practicing these four noble principles we can walk on this path of perfection (Ihsan). Cheikh Ahmadou Bamba said that Ihsan (good character/perfection) is Sufism.

Love and light---sufi

127

786... If your knowledge of fire has been turned to certainty by words alone, then seek to be cooked by the fire itself. Don't abide in borrowed certainty. There is no real certainty until you burn; if you wish for this, sit down in the fire. Mathnawi, Maulana Jallaluddin Rumi, may Allah sanctify his soul & bless his secret.

128

The illusion of finding a wife

786...a good friend has asked me about desire and finding a wife. The only "good" desire is the desire for Allah. This to must be overcome at the end of the journey. In reality "you" are not alone because "you" do not exist. Allah is alone because only Allah is real, has existence... where is this wife to be found that is separate from "you" or Allah? She does not exist. When you find her, it will be Allah you have found. In her you will see your self, and ultimately come to know Allah through unity with "her". My cheikh has said, "Allah put his secret inside the woman."

Our Beloved Prophet Muhammad, alay he salam, has said, "marriage is half of Islam." The true marriage is the union of the soul (feminine) with the spirit (masculine). This union must take place inside the heart of every traveler on this path. Without the union of these two principles, soul/spirit, there can be no Self Realization...

.... love and light---sufi

Ya Latif (129x) after every salat is a for Tarqiya of the soul 786... advice during trials of the lower self.

Insha Allah i will try to call you tonight... i want you to know that you are one of the best friends, and brothers that i have known in this life. You have a sincerity about you that is rare, even amongst the Muslims.... Brother, take care of yourself. You are more important than you know. The light that you have will affect your family, and the future... i love you, and only wish the best for you. You must fight your lower self and desires. Try to purify yourself of all bad habits, and detrimental actions.... i know you have the strength and fortitude to defeat your lower self... The true warrior of light is the warrior that can defeat all of the internal enemies. When all of the internal enemies have been defeated, there is no external enemy that can harm you...

A sufi sister once said to me "life is easy, but we choose to make it difficult." Many people have being saying to me, sufi, I do not have peace in my life. What can I do to have peace in my life? The only way to have peace in your life is to develop an inner state of "peace" that you take with you into the world. The world will not give you peace. **Each of us must develop an internal state of peace that is unshakeable by the storms of the world.** This Internal state of peace must be "cultivated." It is cultivated by daily spiritual practice, and the gradual turning of consciousness inwardly to the Divine instead of outwardly to objects and situations. If you do not have a practice that gives you peace, and turns your consciousness inward to the Divine, please ask, and we will help guide you in the sufi way of peace and transcendence... love and light---sufi`

130

786... Expansion and Contraction

On this exalted path of return to Oneness, all travelers will experience the alternating states know as expansion (Basit) and contraction (Qabid). You must know which of the states you are in, and the proper conduct (adab) for the state. A balloon that is full of air can be used to represent expansion, and a balloon that has very little, or no air represents contraction. The state of expansion is characterized by affluence, abundance, and outward expansion in one's life. The state of contraction is characterized by poverty, constraint, and isolation from people. In the state of expansion the traveler should show gratitude and thankfulness to the Divine, and be careful of feeling of pride, arrogance and forgetfulness. In the state of contraction the traveler should show patience in adversity, and hope for an Opening from the Divine. It is said in the sufi way that the state of contraction is a blessing, and the state of expansion is a test...You will know the blessing of your contraction from your experience in expansion...it is the pressure contraction that creates the diamond. For a better explanation of this concept, and the sufi path, please read "The Book of Wisdom"(Al-Hikam) by Ibn Atala...

love and light---sufi

131

You don't speak French sufi? It will be easier for me! Perhaps you don't know the French system. Here, we have a lot of associations, which give food to the homeless, and it's a fight one over one to have subsided from the French government!! I try to find a homeless, not in my city but in Paris! I found two and I asked them if they want to eat and they said me no! In France, we have a lot of care for homeless! The only thing i can do, it's to keep a generous heart and if i meet a homeless, to feed him! Incha'Allah! May Allah help your action! Victor

People Feeding People

786... Food For Thought is "People Feeding People." It is just that simple. Just imagine, what if some people from all over the world decided to feed some homeless and needy people once a month on the last Saturday of each month? That is just what happened!!! Imagine 8 cities in America and 4 countries over sea's feeding people on the same day... What a Blessing. What a Beautiful way to share with others!!!

God willing the first Food For Thought is this Saturday. We are working on putting up a page for the participants in the different cities and countries to post their experiences. This page should be up soon.

If you want to participate it is not too late. All you have to do is cook some food and give it away! It is not rocket science.... May the Light of the Heavens and the Earth Bless all who participate in these days of sharing....

Love and light----sufi

132

786... So you want to pray 5 times a day. Salat (the Islamic prayer) is to deep for an email, but i bet if you type in "how to make salat" on the net, many self-help sites will come up...after you do that. Feel free to ask me any questions about the specifics. As you know there are 5 prayers a day, but don't try to start with all five everyday. Try to do the first prayer when you wake up, and the one just before going to sleep first. Then when you can do this for 40days, try to add one more salat. Keep doing this until you are in the habit of making all 5. It will be easier for you like this... in the Quran Allah says, "Islam is revealed in stages." love and light---sufi

133

786. . . . I have a dream, the sufi version I have a dream that one day the KKK will change their uniform colors to red black and green, listen to Bob Marley, smoke a big rasta blunt, and say we love all people!!! That one day, the president will tell the truth, and that one day this country will live in peace beyond the walls of racism. I have a dream that one day, people will stop fighting about God, and come to know that they are That which they are fighting over!!! Love and light---sufi

134

786... Food for Thought is "people feeding people." It is simple, cook food, give it away! It is not rocket science people. So far we have 12 cities and 4 different countries that are helping. From California to New York. From France, to Russia. There is also a sister in the state of Washington who is going to get some teenagers to help her with the project!!! You go girl! No one knows the Blessings of one good deed!!!!! Anyway it is not too late if you want to participate. All you have to do is, guess what? Cook some food and give it away to a homeless person/people on the last Saturday of each month. This is going to be a group effort, in different cities on the same day!!! The first day is going to be Saturday (God willing). It would be nice if we had a place to post/share are experiences in different cities each month. If anyone has time to create a group called "Food for Thought" - people feeding people, let me know. Also our sufi study group in Philadelphia is accepting new students. We meet once a week... Love and Light---sufi

135

786... Sufism was once a practice without a name. Now it is a name without a practice. The Prophet Muhammad (peace and light be upon him) was the Highest sufi to ever walk this earth. During that time it was not called sufism. It was called tassawuf, or tazkiyah tul nafs (purification of the soul). Our beloved prophet Muhammad was given 3 teachings from Allah. The first he taught to everyone (shariat). The second (tariqat) he gave only to a few of his companions. The third level (haqiqat), he did not teach to anyone, but buy practicing the second branch of knowledge, the third level, can be opened to you on the inside. The Quran says "fear Allah and Allah will teach you." this is the third level of inner knowledge... during the prophet's time there was a group of poor people that lived in the Mosque. He taught them this second level of knowledge. These people lived on a certain bench/sofa in the mosque. The Arabic word for bench is (suf), thus these people were later called "the people of the bench", or sufi...if you want to start on the sufi path, i will help you insha Allah... love and light---sufi

136

786..."in this book is a healing."-Al Quran... Do you know Ayatul Kursi (the verse of the throne) in the Quran? It is verse 255 in the second chapter. This is a heavy dose of medicine. It may take a while. If you memorize it, and recite it often it will remove your panic attacks. If you ever feel one coming on, it has the power to push it away. This time i wanted to give you "real" medicine, and not a small band-aid. It sounds like you really need to get over these panic attacks. First you can learn it in English, and then in Arabic. It will take some time. This verse is the most powerful verse in the Quran and it can be used for many things. Once you have it memorized let me know, and insha Allah i will give you some secret uses of it! ps. How are you coming along with the zikr i gave you? Are you ready for more?????? love and light---sufi

137

786... Light upon Light... From your words we can tell that you have what we call in sufism "himma"/spiritual attraction for Divinity. My cheikh said that the only thing he cannot give a diciple is Himma. With your Himma, and a little guidance on the sufi path, insha Allah (if it is the will of Allah) you will be able to "arrive". In sufism, arrival is death/extinction in the Divine while still on this plane of existence. Arrival is existence in ONENESS beyond the veil of duality created by the mind. The name that can be named is not the eternal name. The true Way does not have a name. We say sufism, or Tao to describe the process of Self Realization, but it is beyond "religion" names, and form. "Emptiness is form. Form is emptiness."-The Buddha. We must empty the heart of all forms, so that the heart may take the "form" of the Divine. "The secret of Allah is man. The secret of man is Allah."-Bawa Muhaiyadeen... we have been given the true way by a true master, is there any ONE that wants to drink, and become intoxicated????? love and light---sufi

138

786... Sending prayers on the prophet Muhammad is one of the best ways to raise the station of a sufi. It is said that sending blessing on the prophet is the cheikh of one who does not have a cheikh!!! **Salatul Fati** 174x a day brings wealth and prosperity! Allah-hu-ma-sali-ala-Saydi-na-Muhammad-al-fati-hi-li-ma-ug-li-ka. wal-kati-mi-li-ma-sa-ba-ka. nasi-ril-haqi-bil-haqi. wal-Hadi-ee-la-sirat-ti-kal-moos-ta-keem. wa-ala-ali-hi-haq-qad-qad-ri-he-wal-mik-dar-re-hil-athem...

Many tears are shed for the Beloved Light of the two worlds, Nabi Muhammad, the rose in the rose garden, the scent of the Beloved, guide of the lost, opener of the way, sea of mystery, seal of the messengers, may eternal peace, light, and blessings be upon him, and all who follow him, until the day of judgment, and beyond.... tears, tears, and more tears.... Ya Muhammad, Ya Habib, salam alaika!! ---love and light---sufi

139

786...."Meet Joe Black"-Death is watching!!!...Recently i was over one of my sufi friends house that has a TV!!! Imagine that, a sufi with a TV... The movie Meet Joe Black was on. After one scene i was captivated. The angel of death had taken a human form and had fallen in love with a women. The woman was also in love with him, but did not know that he was the angel of death. Now, i ask the question, how many of us are in love with death? The very things that we love can often cause the death of the heart, spirituality, and even physical death. Believe it or not the angel of death is watching you. The angel of death visits every person 5 times a day at the times of prayer... Have you ever visited the cemetery? If not, one day you will. Will you be ready?

Just as death is certain, life after death is certain. There is no death for the soul! You will live in a new form in a new world that will be based on your actions in this world... So it is important that you live in the Light here, so you will not be in the dark there.... Try to think about your death. Will you walk into the Light??? love and light---sufi

786... as salam alaikum, you have asked a good question. This is from a Hadith from our Beloved Nabi Muhammad, eternal peace be upon him "die before you die." It has several meanings. Die before you die means the death of your human traits and the birth of the Divine attributes of Allah in you, on the plane of the soul. First of all we must die to the desires of the nafs (lower self). We must die to following our will and follow only the will of Allah... When we do this, we become "dead" to our own self, and alive in the All Living Allah. Death before death is a gradual process. With the help of a true Cheikh and the Mercy of Allah it is possible. In sufism there are three stages of fana (death/extinction): death in the cheikh, death in the Prophet, and ultimately death in Allah... Enough cannot be said on this topic... The first step of the diciple is extinction (fana) in the teacher... Only Allah can lead you to a true master. It is Allah that gives true guidance through a true master. Allah's attribute of Al Hadi (The Guide) will be manifest to the True seeker when they make the firm, pure intention to "RETURN" to Allah. It is a part of the destiny of a true seeker, to meet a true master/teacher based on the students intentions and sincerity. When the student is ready the teacher will appear. Yes, on the path it is possible to have more than one teacher... It depends on the level of the cheikhs that you meet... A teacher can only take you as far as they have traveled. If Allah Blesses you to meet One who has "arrived," then you will Arrive with His or Her instructions... May Allah guide you to Himself, through a True Master, Hu/who is the manifestation of the inner reality/potential of the seeker.... let me Breath a little...Man is a Divine Being of Light. We are not humans as we have been taught in the west. The teachings of birth and death are false. The soul is an Eternal Light that can NEVER be separate from Allah. Allah in His Divine Mercy manifest Himself through a Living Master in order to guide the True seekers of the Light back to Himself...the great Sufi Master Ibn Arabi has said "Allah sent Himself to Himself with Himself." this is the great secret. Only Allah/Yaheweh/Brahman/God exists...the Reality of Allah in eminent and transcendent. Without meeting the Divine in Human form it is impossible to reach the transcendent Reality. It is through the Master that the seeker finds the true path to Self Realization...the Master is the outer Manifestation of the inner potential of the seeker. Allah sent Himself to Himself with Himself... one love and light...sufi

786..."be still and Know that I am God."---The Bible when we learn to still the mind we can know God. God is a Light inside of your heart. In reality you are one with that Light..."Allah is the Light of the heavens and the earth."--The Quran. The heavens represents the mind, and the earth represents the body/the heart.... meditation made easy: sit facing the east 2 times a day and say: **Laa ee la ha ill Allah** for 10 minutes. It means: God is the only One worthy of worship. It also means God is the only reality. At the end of the 10 minutes say: **Muhammad dur rasool lu la**. 1 time it means: Muhammad is a prophet of God.

After one week of practice, extend the time period to 20min. at the end of the third week extend the time to 30minutes. If done twice a day, over time, this will begin to purify your heart and you mind... When this becomes easy let me know. Also it is good to burn some type of incense during the meditation... A sufi is meditation in motion. Try to find a way to take your meditation with you wherever you go, repeat the meditation in your mind at al times. This is the goal, to be in Union with God.... love and light---sufi

142

Can You tell me about the Sufi ways? I would be very Honored.

786... The way of the sufi is the way of the Lovers of God. The sufi path is the path of unification with God through Love. God is Love. In loving only God we become one with God. In loving only God we love all of creation because in sufi philosophy, God is the only Reality that exist. In loving God we "die daily" as it says in the bible, so that God can live through us. In loving God we serve others, because in serving others, we are serving God... My beloved cheikh said to me "the only one closer to God than you, is the one who Loves God more than you." this is the way of the sufi.... love and light---sufi

143

786... Someone asked me about Love... Love is a flame that i lost my self in a long time ago... Since my entrance into the flame of love, i have not seen my self. All i see is the Beloved.... In fact, i died in the flame of Love.... sufi

144

786... yes, yes, yes. There is a cure for panic attacks. Allah says in the Quran "surely by the remembrance of Allah/God, hearts are made tranquil." You should say the meditation: la-ee-la-ha-ill-Allah as much as possible. This will put your heart at rest. When you feel an attack coming try to breath slow, and say this meditation inwardly. It has two meanings: 1.there is no worthy of worship but God. 2. God is the only reality you must try to know your true Self. Lower negative emotions are from the false self, and a false since of insecurity. The true Self is beyond any harm, it is even beyond death!!! Hu-wal-Hayy (He is the Living)...remember Allah and He will remember you. Allah is As-Salam (the source of Peace.) peace on mind/heart come from Allah...love and light---sufi

145

786... My mother, may Allah put more light in her grave, used to say, "fear is false evidence appearing real." Fear is from the lower self; it comes from a low since of Iman/faith in Allah. If we truly understood that Allah was in total control of all, we would not have fear. Allah is the only power in the universe. We will never be able to please everyone, so do not have fear of others opinion of you. On the Day of Judgment, you will not think about these others, so do not waste you energy on them now. Focus on Allah, and His happiness with you. In the Quran Allah says, "have you seen those who neither fear nor grieve." He says this as if it is a rare state that we must seek for. A life beyond fear and grief...there is a zikr that can help you over come fear and increase your Iman in Allah. The zikr is: haas-be-ya-la-hu-wa-nee-mal-wakil:

(Allah is sufficient for me, in Allah i trust.)

When this zikr was given to me, the prescription was 200x after each salat, but i do not know how much time you have for zikr after salat. Continue with the first zikr i gave you, and add this zikr 11x after each salat....

as salam alaikum, love and light----sufi

Al Faqir – Spiritual Poverty

786... Sidi Ahmad Zaruq, may Allah be pleased with him, has said, "the sufi is the one who strives to sift his time of everything but the Truth. If he eliminates everything but the Truth from himself, then he is a man of spiritual poverty (al-faqir)."

This is the true meaning of spiritual poverty. On this path of asceticism, we often think that less is more, and we equate this less to material things. This is a mistake because our beloved Nabi Muhammad, may eternal peace, light, and blessings be upon him has said "the hand facing down is better than the hand facing up". This means, "the hand that gives is better than the hand that receives." This denotes that our spiritual poverty is not related to material things. Thus our spiritual poverty should involve the removal of everything but Allah, and His attributes from our being.

It is very easy to give up everything and move to a cave. It is very difficult to remove everything from the cave of the heart. May we all strive for this exalted state of Al-Faqir, the true spiritually poor. Love and Light---sufi

147

786... The Checker Board of Life

This is the world of duality. We will travel on squares of light and squares of darkness. You will only know the power of the Light when you travel in the Darkness. Let your light shine, and know that the darkness is an Illusion. My grandfather may Allah Bless his grave with Light, used to say "it does not matter what happens to you in life. What matters is how you react to what happens." We all experience the same drama/dance of light and darkness. The Hindu's call it the Divine Dance of Shiva. Example: two peoples parents die from cancer. One person turns to alcohol and drugs because of the pain, the next person devotes his life to fighting cancer by working with youth smoke prevention programs. Same drama, different reaction. This is the drama of life. In a dark room when you turn the Light on what happens??????? Keep the Light on, even if you have to borrow money to pay the bill....

Love and Light-----sufi

148

786...."Hu wal Tawab ur Raheem."-Quran He is the Merciful, Accepter of Repentance... Be sure that on this path of Haqq (truth), there will be downfalls. Allah is all forgiving. He loves forgiving His servants. It is said that if there were no more sin in the world, Allah would create some people, who would sin, just so He could forgive them. Don't ever feel that you are beyond the power of Allah's forgiveness. This is a trick of satan. A saint is a sinner who got up one more time than he feel. Sin can be used as fuel, and inspiration to fight against our lower self. Make the best of your situation. Ask Allah for forgiveness, and put the sword of zikr and fasting to your lower self... love and light---sufi

149

786... To be a giver and receiver of light, you must find a way to be with the people of LIGHT... i don't know which city you are in, but there must be some sufis "people of LIGHT" there. Try to find them.... and become like them... This is the easiest way. The sufis say "if you stay close to the rose garden, one day you will start to smell like a rose".... Start with saying: LAA EE LA HA ILL ALLAH... as much as you can. This will begin to purify you and give you light. When the light inside you builds up, it will draw you to the people of light on the outside that you need to be with. It will also push the darkness of illusion away from you.... love and light---sufi

150

786... as salam alaikum dear traveler on the path of Al Haqq. As I am sure that you know in the hadith our Beloved Habib Allah, Nabi Muhammad, the greatest of all creation, light of the two worlds, may peace, blessings and light be upon Him eternally, has said " Ihsan is to worship Allah as if you see Him. And if you can't see Him know that Allah see's you." Cheikh Ahmadou Bamba has said that ihsan is the perfection of Iman and Islam, and that to have ihsan we must have purity of heart and sincerity in action. We cultivate ihsan by always being aware "conscious" of Allah. Ihsan is consciousness of Allah at all times. The distraction of the world prevents us from developing ihsan. Just as the living prophet is the straight way, the living cheikh is the straight way for his disciples. When we follow the cheikh, we will be walking in the footsteps of the Rasool alay hi salam. love and light----sufi

151

786... Today the question was asked, "what is the true character of a sufi." This was our answer ... ... wa laikum as salam... A True sufi is one who practices the sunnah of the Beloved Prophet Muhammad, alay hi salam, with a different intention. We worship Allah Because He is worthy of worship, not in order to go to Jannah/heaven. We worship Allah seeking His Divine Proximity; to be of those who are the foremost in the eye's of Allah. We practice the sunnah of the prophet with extra (nafl) acts of worship to purify our souls. There are 7 stations of the soul. Most people never make it past the second level. My cheikh, Cheikh Ahmadou Bamba said, "if it is not in the Holy Quran or the Hadith's it is not from me." In Islam we have: shariat, tariqat, haqiqat and marifat. The shariat is just the beginning of the path... If you want to learn sufism, you should find a True living cheikh, that follows the Holy Quran and Sunnah, and learn the path of tariqat from him or her. love and light-sufi

152

786... Once when i was sitting with my Cheikh in Senegal, i looked at him and said "Cheikh Betcio, i don't want to go to heaven." My beloved Cheikh looked at me and said, "I don't want to go either." Then he went on to explain the Divine Proximity of Allah, which he explained, is Beyond Heaven. In the Holy Quran in Surah Waqia Allah describes three groups in the next life/world: the people on the left, the people on the right, and the foremost. It is this group, the foremost, that the sufi tries to be with, in the Divine Proximity of Allah. It was the great sufi Cheikh Abdul Qadir Jilani who said, " i studied the heavens and found a flaw in heaven. Heaven is not eternal. It was at this point that i turned my face towards that which is eternal, Allah." He, may Allah grant him more Light from Nur Muhammad (alay hi salam) also said "sufism is two steps, one step out of this world into the next world/heaven, and one step out of the next world/heaven into the Divine Presence." My cheikh said that the difference between the Divine Presence and heaven is greater than the difference between heaven and hell...heaven is the hell of the sufi. Cheikh Ahmadou Bamba said, "heaven is for my lazy disciple." May we all seek for the Divine Presence.... love and light-sufi

153

786..."When you melt, dissolving in the Unity Ocean of Allah Almighty then you may understand the meaning of "Fani-Fillah" (Annihilation in Allah). When you abandon your position as a being in existence, when you become as a drop of rain falling from the sky and are immersed, united in that Ocean of Divine Unity, then no one can ask where that drop has gone: the drop became an Ocean." SubhanAllah   - beloved Maulana Cheikh Nazim- sultan ul Awlia

154

786.... Islam is an ocean. Most people only make it to the beach, and never enter the ocean of Islam...Islam is the first step. Then comes Iman. Then Ihsan.... Ihsan is the pearl at the bottom of the ocean of Islam that only the sufi dives deep enough to find. Islam is a matter of the heart. Not the mind. Ihsan is self-realization and perfection. Cheikh Ahmadou Bamba said that Islam and Iman are made perfect by Ihsan. Without Ihsan, Islam does not have life...Ihsan is sufism...love and light---sufi

155

786...Finding Self Here a certain question arises: how does the person who has the aptitude for the state of gnosis understand his own reality! It is answerable in this way: It is necessary that he finds a gnostic who knows his own self and after he has found him, from the bottom of his heart, and with all his soul, make his character to be his character. The person of gnosis, to find his own origin, should hold on to this way and the following Quranic verse points to this meaning: "Search for the means that will take you to Him." The explanation of this may be as follows: There are of My servants those who have found Me. If you want to find Me follow in their footsteps. They become a means for you and they finally lead to Me. If this is so then by serving those people, a person comes to know himself. He will understand whence he came and where he is going and he will have an inkling of the station of the present state. ...165

156

786... Prem Hotep, Dear Self, there are as many paths to Self Realization as there are people. Without a Self Realized Master it is impossible to reach Self Realization. The path that we are walking is the sufi path. After studying many different paths, the seeker must choose one direct path and devote herself to that path under the direct guidance of a Living Master. In reality, it does not matter which path you choose, if your Master is Self Realized, she will guide you safely across the dessert/hell of the lower self... We pray that Allah bless you with a true Master... Which path are you walking on? love and light-sufi

157

786... That is very good. If you are a Baptist be a true Baptist. Try to be as much like Jesus (peace be upon him) as you can. My religion is Love. i love all people that Believe in God. It does not matter to me what a persons religion is. What matters to me is the Love, worship, and belief in God, no matter what name you call Her/Him by... This one God lives in the hearts of all people, no matter what religion, or race they are. God is a Living God, and the giver of Life. God gives all of us Life. Much love to you and yours.

Smile --------one love-sufi

158

786... In answer to a friends question... It is said on the sufi path, "if you do not have a living master, then the devil (lower self) is your master." Without a living master it is impossible to reach Self Realization. It is impossible to read some books and think you can over come your Lower Self from book learning. The master is all-important. We in the west do not like to hear this teaching because we are taught to doubt all and everything. In the east this is a common teaching for those on the Path. Imagine a Hindu without a Guru, or a Buddhist with out a Living Buddhist teacher???? Can you become a doctor without someone teaching you how to be a doctor? None of us in the west would let a doctor operate on us who did not go to medical school. The teacher is the "doctor" for the soul...

One love-sufi

159

786... dear friend Let me first say that to know your Higher Self, is to Know God. Knowing God is the most important thing in Life. Without Knowing God life is a waste of time, a mere dream, in the deep sleep of unknowing. You must seek the way to Know God. Even the Bible says, "straight is the gate, narrow is the way, and few be they that find it." The way must be searched for. Believe me, few find the true way... Our cheikh, Cheikh Ahmadou Bamba teaches that there are four enemies on the path to Knowing God. They are: nafs (the lower self/soul), hawa (passions/desire), dunya (the world), and shaytan (devil)... In his teaching he gives us a clear path to overcome these four enemies. It would take toooo much to explain all this in one letter... So we will stop here and insha Allah (God willing) continue in the future... May the Peace, Light, and Mercy of Allah be with you, and please we ask you to start your search for the path... one love-sufi

160

786... Enough cannot be said on this topic... The first step of the diciple is extinction (fana) in the teacher... Only Allah can lead you to a true master. It is Allah that gives true guidance through a true master. Allah's attribute of Al Hadi (The Guide) will be manifest to the True seeker when they make the firm, pure intention to "RETURN" to Allah. It is a part of the destiny of a true seeker, to meet a true master/teacher based on the students intentions and sincerity. When the student is ready the teacher will appear. Yes, on the path it is possible to have more than one teacher... It depends on the level of the cheikhs that you meet... A teacher can only take you as far as they have traveled. If Allah Blesses you to meet One who has "arrived," then you will Arrive with His or Her instructions...may Allah guide you to Himself, through a True Master, Hu/who is the manifestation of the inner reality/potential of the seeker.... as salam alaikum--- one love-sufi

161

786... Another question from today... One of my teachers, Abdallah Fahmi, said to me, "a good question is half the answer"... The path is "changing our habits." If we do not leave our houses we will not change our habits. It is good to travel. In sufism the path is called "tariqat". Tariqat is an Arabic word that means pathway/travel.... sufism is the science of the purification of the soul through various methods. In the Egyptian Book of the dead it is said that when the ka (soul) and the ba (spirit) are united the student becomes God/Divine. It is the same in sufi teaching. The soul must be purified in order to unite/yoga with the spirit. The soul is light, and the spirit is light. At the time of birth, which is actually death, the soul forgets its identity. During our life, the things we experience cover the soul in darkness...sufism returns the soul to its original state of purity.......... be safe in India, if you do not have a living master, you may be led to one in India...love light--- sufi

162

786... as salam alaikum... May the Peace of Allah, your True Self, be with you. The Self Is All. All is The Self. The Divine Self manifested on this plane of duality to Know It Self. All Is One. Duality is an illusion created by the mind and the false since of "i". There is no "i" separate from Allah. "Hu am I." Allah is Allah. Allah is All. The only Reality that exists is One. This One is your True Self. Wake up from the dream of a false since of separateness from the Divine. If you do not find Allah in your Self, you will never find Allah. If you do not Know Allah as your True Self, you will never Know Allah. Allah/God/Brahman/Yahweh are all names of your True Self. Die before you die, the way of the –sufi

163

On the authority of Abu Harayrah (may Allah be pleased with him), who said that the Prophet (PBUH) said: Allah the Almighty said: I am as My servant thinks I am. I am with him when he makes mention of Me. If he makes mention of Me to himself, I make mention of him to Myself; and if he makes mention of Me in an assembly, I make mention of him in an assemble better than it. And if he draws near to Me an arm's length, I draw near to him a fathom's length. And if he comes to Me walking, I go to him at speed.

Hadith Qudsi 15 - It was related by al-Buhkari (also by Muslim, at-Tirmidi and Ibn-Majah).

164

786... Then one day, as he sat in the presence of Moulay Abdusalam who had his young son on his knees playing and enjoying himself, the thought came to him to ask him about the Greatest Name of Allah. He said that at that moment the child who sat on his father's knees put his hands on his shoulders and shook him, saying, "O Abul Hassan, you want to ask about the Greatest Name of Allah. It is of no importance to ask about the Greatest Name of Allah. It is important that you should be the Greatest Name of Allah." When his son had finished speaking, the master smiled and said, "Such a one has answered you for me." Four fundamental themes ran through the teaching of Moulay Abdusalam to Abul Hassan, as perceived from his famous Hizb, called as-Salat al-Mashishiya: The Oneness of Existence (wahdat al-wujud) which he said could be realized only through asceticism, fear of God and His judgments (khawfu billah), the belief that God is everywhere and that it is necessary to see His Face in everything that He has created, and fourthly, that only through the drowning in the Ocean of the Unity (awnu fi bahri al-wahadati) can the seeker cast off and leave behind his own existence and attributes to be merged and absorbed into Allah and His Attribute.

165

786... sufi KEY Durood Taj for those seeking Divine proximity.

Durood Taj

Ya Allah! Send down Rahmat (Mercy) upon our Master and Chief, Muhammad, the Crowned One (with the kingdom of both worlds), and the One with Mi'raj (Ascension), and the Owner of Buraq (Mount of Light), and the Banner.

(He is, by Allah's Permission) the Repeller of Calamities and Epidemics, and Famine, and Disease, and Agony.

His Name is inscribed and made prominent and made Worthy of Intercession, and is engraved as such in the Loh and Qalam (Preserved Tablet and Pen).

He is the Chief of Arabs and non-Arabs. His Body is All Holy, Perfumed, and Purified, Illuminated in the Sacred Houses, and Kabba.

He is a Shining Sun (Duha, Rising Sun), and full Moon dispelling Darkness, a Refuge for all beings, and a Lamp (of Guidance) in the Darkness (of ignorance and paganism).

He is the Best in Adab (Conduct), Intercessor of Ummahs (Communities), blessed with Eminence, Generosity.

And Allah is his Protector, Jibril (Gabriel) is his Attendant, the Buraq (Mount of Light) is his Mount, and Mi'raj (Ascension) is his Journey, and Sidratul Muntaha is his Station.

He desires Kabba Kaussain, and his desire is his Objective, and his Objective he has realized.

He is Syed (Chief) of all the Messengers, and the Last One of the Nabees, intercessor of the Sinners, a Refuge of the Homeless, and he is a Mercy of all the Worlds.

He is the Aspiration of the Aspirers.

He is Shams (Sun) of the Arifeen, and is the Light of Guidance for the Saliheen (people on the Path), and he is the Guide of those

seeking Proximity with Allah (Annihilation unto Allah):
Mukarabeen.

A Lover of Fuqra, and poor and destitute, the Chief of Jinn and Mankind, the Nabi of two Haramain, Imam of Two Qiblahs.

He is our Refuge here and in the Hereafter, and His Station is Kabba Kaussain, being the Beloved of the Rabb (Lord) of the Easts and Wests.

He is the Grandfather of Hassan and Hussain (ra), He is our Master, and of all Jinn and Mankind, Abu L Qasim, Muhammad bin Abdullah!

And Nur (Light) from the Nur (Light) of Allah!

Ye Lovers of the Beauty of his Nur (Light)!

Send Durood and Salaams (Peace) upon him, and his Descendants, and his Companions!

AMEEN

Durood--Taj

Transliteration:

Allahumma salli `ala sayyidina wa mawlana Muhammadin sahibit taji wal-mi`raji wal-buraqi wal-`alam. Dafi` al-bala'i wal-waba'i wal-qahti wal-maradi wal-alam. ismuhu maktubum marfu`um mashfu`um manqushun fil lawhi wal-qalam. Sayyidil `arabi wal-`ajam. Jismuhu muqaddasum mu`attarum mutahharum munawwarun fil-bayti wal-haram. Shamsid duha badrid duja sadril `ula nuril huda kahfil wara misbahiz zulam. Jamilish shyami shafi` il-umam. Sahibil judi wal-karam. Wallahu `asimuhu. Wa jibrilu khadimuhu. Wal-buraqu markabuhu. Wal-mi`raju safaruhu wa sidratul -muntaha maqamuhu. Wa qaba qawsayni matlubuhu. Wal-matlubu maqsuduhu wal-maqsudu mawjuduh. Sayyidil mursalin. Khatimin nabiyyeena shafi`il mudhnibin. Anisil gharibeena rahmatil lil `alamin. Rahatil `ashiqeen. Muradil mushtaqeen. Shamsil `arifeen. Sirajis salikeen Misbahil muqarrabeen. Muhibbil fuqara'ay wal-ghuraba'ay wal-masakeen. Sayyidith thaqalaynay nabiyyil haramayn. imamil qiblatayn. Waseelatina fid darayn. Sahibi qaba qawsayni mahbubi rabbil mashriqayni wal-maghribayn. Jadd al-hasani wal-husayn mawlana wa mawlath thaqalayn Abil Qasimi MUHAMMAD ibn `Abdillahi nurinm min nurillahi yaa ayyuhal mushtaquna bi nuri jamalihi sallu `alayhi wa alihi wa ashabihi wa sallimu taslima.

Made in the USA
Middletown, DE
11 August 2023

36485794R00104